The Official
CHASE
'N YUR FACE
Cookbook

Text © 2016 Chase 'N Yur Face Media LLC
Photography © 2016 Jessica-Nicosia Nadler
Chapter Openers and Fun Fact Illustrations © 2016 Chase 'N Yur Face Media LLC
Interior Line Art Illustrations © Shutterstock

ISBN-13: 978-0-692-75585-3

Library of Congress Cataloging-in-Publication Data is
available on file.

Published by
Chase 'N Yur Face Media LLC
www.chasenyurface.com

In Association with:

James O. Fraioli
Culinary Book Creations
www.culinarybookcreations.com

Designed by *the*BookDesigners
www.bookdesigners.com

Printed in China through Globalink
www.globalinkprinting.com

10 9 8 7 6 5 4 3 2 1

TASTY RECIPES & FUN FACTS TO START YOUR FOOD ADVENTURE

The Official CHASE 'N YUR FACE Cookbook

CHASE BAILEY

PHOTOGRAPHY BY **JESSICA NICOSIA NADLER**
ILLUSTRATIONS BY **SAMUEL A. BAILEY**

**A CHASE 'N YUR FACE
MEDIA LLC BOOK**

To Papa—my grandfather Edgar E. Bailey Jr.
—*for always encouraging and believing in me,
and for always being proud of me.
I'm going to keep fulfilling my dreams
and making him proud.*

ACKNOWLEDGMENTS

I want to thank the following people and organizations for giving me the inspiration and support to "Make It Happen":

UNCLE SAM – My godfather, for using his artistic talents to help bring the vision to life.

UNCLE EDGAR – For helping me come up with the name "Chase 'N Yur Face."

PETER – For his faith, and his commitment to help me succeed.

AUNT MARGARET – For doing whatever it takes to "get 'er done."

THE FERNALD FAMILY – For standing by me, stepping up, and always showing up for the party.

TATIANA – For spending LOTS of her free time and late nights helping to get the CNYF ball rolling.

DIANE – For being there from the beginning, and believing in me.

SARA – For literally crossing an ocean to make sure the right opportunities come my way.

TAMMI – For handling all those important technical details that the rest of us might miss or don't even know about.

THE HINES FAMILY – For "keepin' it real," being another set of hands when there's work to be done, and being there when I need to take a break and just "chillax."

MATT, WALTER, AND EULIS – For helping me build my confidence and encouraging me to just be myself.

AUTISM SPEAKS – For honoring me with the opportunity to share my journey and gifts at the 2015 Autism Speaks to Los Angeles Celebrity Chef Gala.

CHEF NICK SHIPP – For taking the time to mentor me on how a real restaurant kitchen operates.

JAMES O. FRAIOLI & THE TEAM AT CULINARY BOOK CREATIONS – For their expertise and enthusiasm in guiding me through the process of publishing this cookbook.

And most of all my mom, **MARY BAILEY**, for literally EVERYTHING!

CONTENTS

INTRODUCTION

Before you dive into my recipes and all the other fun and interesting things in my cookbook, I think it's important that you know a little bit about me and my journey. Knowing about my life will help you understand why this cookbook is important to me; even more important, it will encourage you to find out what you want to do with your own life, and go for it!

Let me start by saying that life is full of unexpected challenges, adventures, and even a few miracles along the way. You could say that my pursuing a career in the culinary and entertainment industries is a miracle. See, I was diagnosed with autism when I was a toddler. And like many people with autism, I had *severe* food aversions. For the first few years of my life, I ate only five different food items. But that wasn't the only challenge I faced. My diagnosis also included speech delay and other developmental and physical issues. Some doctors told my mom that I would probably never speak, and would not be able to take care of myself.

But that's not how things turned out for me. I got lucky: I have a mom who is brave, smart, and creative, and who likes adventures as much as I do. She worked hard to make sure I got the help I needed, and created a homeschool curriculum designed especially for me—one that fits who I am, the way I learn, and the goals I have for my life.

To me, having autism means that my brain just works differently from some other people's brains, so I learn and do things in different ways. I learn with my eyes and by doing—watching and repeating things over and over. After I watch things and think about them for a while, I feel comfortable trying them myself. Actually going places and doing the things that I'm learning about helps me understand and remember. Just hearing or reading words without experiences or pictures to reference doesn't work for me, especially when I'm dealing with something new.

I have a process I call "Check It Out, Get Up and Go, Make It Happen." Here's how it works: After I studied colonial America, I took a trip to Philadelphia and Washington, D.C., so that the things I was learning about would be more alive in my mind. When I studied diversity, and conflict management and resolution, I participated in role plays and went to the Simon Wiesenthal Museum of Tolerance. And when I learned about England, I was able to take a trip there to see and do some of the things that I had heard and read about.

The "Check It Out, Get Up and Go, Make It Happen" process is also how I've been able to overcome food aversions. Like I mentioned before, when I was little, I could only eat five foods—all the others really freaked me out. New tastes, smells, and textures were just too much for me to handle. But when I was around eight years old, my grandfather and I used to watch TV after I got home from school, and one day we found a few cooking

shows and decided to check them out. I especially liked a show called *Eat St.*; in fact, I became *obsessed*. I liked cooking shows because I got to watch the chefs and learn about different foods without having to touch, smell, or taste them. The chefs seemed like they were having a great time, and the people eating their food seemed to be really enjoying themselves. Some of the chefs were pretty funny too, and many of them traveled all over the world. These cooking shows helped me to see that food could actually be fun, and a big part of traveling—which is one of my favorite things. I also noticed that many chefs owned their own restaurants and food trucks, which I thought was pretty cool. I started saying to myself, "I think I can do this...I wanna try this." I started imagining how I would change some of the recipes, and even making up some of my own. I also started imagining how I would do my own cooking show.

When I told my mom what I was thinking, she was completely blown away. We started going to different restaurants so I could try new foods, and we started trying new recipes at home, too. I was really pumped about my ideas, and kept talking about them, and one day my mom said, "Why wait until you grow up? Let's do it now!" So with the help of family, friends, and other awesome people, I started my *Chase 'N Yur Face* cooking show on YouTube. At first, it was pretty basic, with just me and my mom filming in a friend's kitchen. Then we got a small film crew to help out, and I invited guest chefs and foodies to come on the show and teach me cooking skills. I was honored to have chef Roy Choi as my very first guest chef.

I really love comedies and making people laugh, so after a while I added some comedy in the episodes to make them more fun. A couple of years later, I added a new series called *Cooking Tips and Tricks for Beginners*, which are quick, sixty-second videos where I share one tip I've learned that has made things better for me in the kitchen, and might help someone else, too. For example, I have trouble with my fine motor skills, which makes cutting and chopping tricky. So I talked about the food processor that I use to make that part of cooking more comfortable for me.

Along the way, my videos and personal story got people's attention. Students and teachers in schools from different parts of the United States have contacted me to let me know that they have been following my story, cooking my recipes, and feeling inspired to be themselves and try new things. I've had the privilege to visit award-winning chefs and restaurants; been featured in newspapers and

magazines; and appeared on TV shows. But I hadn't done a cookbook until now.

While all these great things were happening, I was also creating recipes, and getting more and more ideas for new ones. Eating at different restaurants; a holiday or special occasion; watching chefs; learning about a new food item; a new kitchen tool; and even just being hungry can all inspire recipe ideas for me. I keep a recipe journal with all my ideas in it. So it just made sense for me to start thinking about doing an actual cookbook to share these recipe ideas with others. The videos I make only show a handful of the recipes that I have created. And a recipe can't be enjoyed if people don't know about it, right?

This cookbook is also a way for me to start conversations and communicate with others. For me, food isn't just about overcoming aversions. It has been a way for me to build relationships. It's not easy for me to start conversations with people I don't know. Some people are quick and really good at talking to new people, finding things in common, and figuring out what kinds of things to talk about. I'm the kind of person that needs to think, watch, and become familiar with who people are before I'm really comfortable talking to them. But I have figured out one thing about people for sure—*everyone* has food in common, and that can be a really good place to begin a conversation.

Putting together this cookbook-conversation has been another exciting and challenging experience. I've gotten to do some pretty amazing things on my journey so far, and with each experience I learn more about the industries I love, and what I want for my own career and life. I consider myself in training to be a chef, restaurateur, comedic actor, TV and film producer and director, and philanthropist. The things I do every day get me closer to these goals, and make me feel creative and *alive*. Honestly, I don't think about being autistic, unless someone else mentions it. In my mind, I'm just Chase—I am who I am, and this is how I roll. I want all people, especially those with autism and other challenges, to feel the same way about themselves. I believe every kid should have the opportunities and support to become whatever it is that makes *them* feel alive.

An important thing I've learned about having adventures and achieving dreams is that you *can't* do it all alone. That's what this cookbook is really all about: bringing friends and family together to have fun, learn, try new things, cheer one another on, and accomplish goals. Sure, there's nothing wrong with cooking a meal by yourself, for yourself. But isn't a meal a lot more satisfying when you have someone else there to appreciate it with you? Life is that way, too. So not only will you find simple recipes for every meal of the day here to nourish your body and make your taste buds happy, you'll also discover fun facts and pictures—food to nourish your thoughts and relationships by starting conversations during mealtimes, and to make you curious about people, places, events, and things that you may not have thought about before. You'll even find out a few more things about me.

Ultimately, this cookbook experience will encourage you to celebrate life and be yourself. And at every great celebration there is *food*!

HEY KIDS!

Remember... Before you do anything in the kitchen, always ask your parent's permission. Let's get started!

- Croissants
- Bagels
- Muffins
- Pancakes

Waffles
Sausage
Bacon
bled Eggs

- Bananas
- Pineapp
- Apples

Grapes

- Or

GET UP & GO

I'm a night owl, not a morning person, but breakfast definitely helps me perk up in the morning. Bacon, pancakes, and muffins always perk me up, but I don't like egg dishes - it doesn't matter how you cook them or with what other foods you mix-in. Growing up in the United States where eggs are a staple breakfast item, and other traditional breakfast offerings are pretty limited, the first meal of the day used to be a challenge for me. In Asian countries like Thailand, China, and Japan, they traditionally eat foods for breakfast that we in the Western world consider lunch and dinner foods—stir-fry dishes, fish and rice, and the like. Honestly, that sounds pretty good to me! But realistically, in my life it would be difficult. I have to find foods and make recipes that appeal to me using the ingredients that are available to me, and ones that my friends and family also enjoy eating for breakfast.

The recipes here get me more excited about breakfast, and they don't take a lot of time to make. Breakfast sandwiches, hot cereal, and sweet and savory muffins are some of the items included on my morning menu, and I hope you'll be adding them to your menu as well.

FUN FACT Did you know that in Europe during the Middle Ages, only poor laborers, sick people, the elderly, and small children were allowed to eat breakfast? Everyone else was expected to be strong enough to wait until lunch; some religious leaders even considered eating breakfast to be a sin of gluttony for healthy people. But in modern times, we know that everyone needs nutrition in the morning, to give our bodies the energy boost we need to face the day. Doctors and scientists consider breakfast the most important meal because it affects how we think, feel, make decisions, and interact with others, as well as our physical activity for the rest of the day. Eating breakfast gets our metabolism working properly and helps us burn calories throughout the day. If we don't eat breakfast, our bodies feel tired and desperate for energy, so we might end up overeating or eating the wrong things when we finally do eat. So make breakfast an important part of your day, and make it something to look forward to with the following dishes. They're simple, delicious, and hearty, and they'll put a smile on your face.

BANANA COCONUT CEREAL

GLUTEN-FREE

Rice cereal is a food I was never interested in eating. But my mom always encourages me to get my nutrients from a variety of foods, and to think about how I can turn something that's healthy, but not very appealing, into something delicious. For instance, mashed potatoes aren't anything to get excited about without all the "good stuff," right? Well, the same is true of rice cereal: You gotta dress it up to really enjoy it. So give this recipe a try and see what you think.

SERVES 1

¾ cup hot rice cereal (or plain oatmeal)
1 tablespoon coconut milk
½ medium-sized banana
½ teaspoon sugar or stevia (optional)
4–5 fresh raspberries, for garnish
2 fresh mint leaves, for garnish

To make the hot rice cereal, follow the instructions on the package.
Note: You can substitute plain oatmeal for rice cereal.

In a bowl, add ¾ cup of the warm rice cereal. Stir in the coconut milk. Use a fork to smash up the banana, then stir it into the cereal mixture. Stir in the sugar or stevia, if desired. Garnish with raspberries and mint leaves. Serve warm.

FUN FACT

Hot cereals are also known as porridge, and like most other foods, porridges have their own championship contests. The World Porridge Making Championship has been held in Carrbridge, Cairngorms National Park, Scotland, since 1994, and World Porridge Day is October 10. The events are held to raise money for the Mary's Meals charity in Argyle, Scotland, which supplies food to children in Africa.

BARNYARD BREAKFAST MUFFINS

GLUTEN FREE (IF MADE WITH GLUTEN FREE CORNMEAL)

Not in the mood for sweet breakfast muffins? Then whip-up these savory sausage corn bread muffins instead. The red pepper flakes and green chilies add a little heat and spice to your morning, while the sausage makes it feel more like a meal. If you don't care for sausage, you can use bacon, diced ham, or any vegan meat substitute. This is a great muffin to make the night before, so all you need to do in the morning is heat it up and go.

MAKES ABOUT 18 MUFFINS

1 package (about 15 ounces) corn bread mix
1 pound ground breakfast turkey sausage
½ cup peeled and chopped yellow onion
½ teaspoon fresh rosemary
1 teaspoon fresh thyme
½ teaspoon red chili pepper flakes
½ cup diced mild green chilies
1 cup shredded cheddar cheese (optional)

Preheat the oven to 350°F.

Line a muffin tin with cupcake liners (or use nonstick spray).

Follow the instructions on the corn bread mix to make a batter, and set it aside.

In a large pan over medium heat, add the turkey sausage, onion, rosemary, thyme, and red pepper flakes. Cook until the sausage is cooked through. Stir in the green chilies. Remove from the heat and add the mixture to the cornbread batter. Add in cheese, if desired. Stir well to combine.

Fill each muffin cup three-quarters of the way full with the mixture. Place the tin in the oven and bake until a toothpick inserted into one of the muffins comes out clean, about 20 to 25 minutes.

FUN FACT
American-style muffins, first made during the eighteenth century, are also called quick breads because they do not require yeast or kneading to rise. Quick bread or American-style muffins are made with a batter, which is softer and thinner than most traditional bread doughs.

PIGS IN A WAFFLE

Sometimes a food that you're sure you won't like and will never eat can taste delicious if it's prepared the right way. This is what happened with me and deli ham. I challenged myself to create a breakfast recipe using ham that I would enjoy eating. The result is a soft, fluffy waffle topped with provolone cheese, honey ham, and a savory-sweet coleslaw, folded in half like a waffle sandwich. Now, this is a waffle done right!

SERVES 4

4 waffles (recipe follows)
8 slices provolone cheese
12 thin slices uncured maple honey ham
2 cups Breakfast Slaw (recipe follows)

On top of one side of a warm waffle, add 2 slices of provolone cheese, 3 slices of ham, and ½ cup Breakfast Slaw. Gently fold one half of the waffle over the other to make a sandwich.

When you're serving this to guests, add a 4-inch toothpick to keep the sandwich closed.

FUN FACT Waffles originated during the Middle Ages in Western Europe. Cooks would pour batter between two metal plates made with a grid pattern to stop the batter from spilling out the sides while it cooked over a fire. In the United States, inventor Cornelius Swartwout patented the first modern-day waffle iron on August 24, 1869. Now August 24 is National Waffle Day in the United States, in honor of Swartwout's patent, while March 25 is International Waffle Day.

WAFFLES

MAKES 4 WAFFLES

1¾ cups flour
¼ cup cornstarch
2 tablespoons sugar
1 tablespoon baking powder
¼ teaspoon salt
2 eggs
1¾ cups milk
½ cup canola oil
2 teaspoons almond extract

Preheat a waffle iron.

In a large mixing bowl, add the flour, cornstarch, sugar, baking powder, salt, eggs, milk, oil, and almond extract. Whisk together until smooth.

Use cooking spray to grease the waffle iron.

Because waffle irons vary in size, follow the instructions for your model to determine how much batter to pour in, and cook the waffle until light golden brown.

BREAKFAST SLAW

SERVES 4

2½ cups roughly shredded green cabbage
½ cup diced Fuji apple
2 teaspoons fresh lemon juice
1½ tablespoons chopped walnuts
1 tablespoon dried blueberries
2–3 tablespoons Ranch Dressing

In a mixing bowl, combine the cabbage, apples, lemon juice, walnuts, blueberries, and Ranch Dressing. Toss well to combine.

SLICE OF EGGCELLENCE
(AKA EGGCELLENCE BREAKFAST PIZZA)

I mentioned at the beginning of this chapter that I'm not a fan of egg dishes, but there are many folks—like my mom—who love them. So this one's for you, Mom! She enjoys subtle and unique flavor combinations, so the eggs and cheese paired with pears and capers on sheepherder's bread is perfect for her. This dish is a meal on its own, but also delicious with a side of bacon, fruit, or hash browns; and it makes a nice presentation for special brunches and breakfast buffets.

MAKES 6-8 PIZZAS, DEPENDING ON THE SIZE OF THE SLICE

1 loaf sheepherder's bread
3 tablespoons melted salted butter
5 eggs
½ cup thin-sliced pears
⅓ cup shredded mozzarella cheese
2 tablespoons capers
Preheat the oven to 400°F.

Cut the top off the sheepherder's bread and remove the center of the loaf, making a deep-dish bread crust, being careful not to tear through the crust. Place it in a deep baking skillet with a lid. Using a pastry brush, brush the inside of the bread crust with butter. Break the eggs into the bread crust, making sure to cover the crust evenly. (If you prefer your eggs scrambled instead of sunny-side up, beat the eggs in a bowl first and then pour into the deep-dish bread crust.) Arrange the pear slices on top of the eggs. If you'd like the dish sweeter, simply add more pears. Sprinkle the cheese on top of the pears.

Place the lid on the skillet and place the skillet in the oven. Set the timer for 20 minutes. After 20 minutes, remove the pan from the oven and sprinkle the top of the dish with the capers. Place back in the oven and bake until the eggs are cooked, about another 15 minutes. Note: If you like the yolks soft, cook for only 5 to 10 additional minutes.

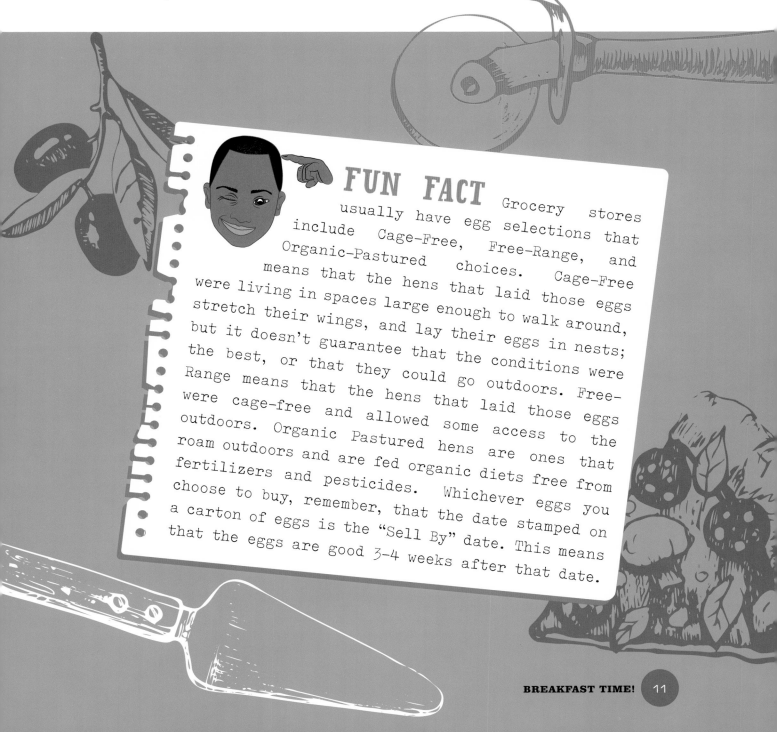

FUN FACT Grocery stores usually have egg selections that include Cage-Free, Free-Range, and Organic-Pastured choices. Cage-Free means that the hens that laid those eggs were living in spaces large enough to walk around, stretch their wings, and lay their eggs in nests; but it doesn't guarantee that the conditions were the best, or that they could go outdoors. Free-Range means that the hens that laid those eggs were cage-free and allowed some access to the outdoors. Organic Pastured hens are ones that roam outdoors and are fed organic diets free from fertilizers and pesticides. Whichever eggs you choose to buy, remember, that the date stamped on a carton of eggs is the "Sell By" date. This means that the eggs are good 3-4 weeks after that date.

SMOKED CHICKEN PANCAKES

(GLUTEN-FREE IF USING GLUTEN-FREE PANCAKE MIX)

I have to admit, pancakes are one of my favorite breakfast foods. They're quick, they're filling, and they leave me feeling happy. How about you? If you answered yes and also like bacon with your pancakes, or enjoy chicken and waffles, then this recipe is definitely for you. Top it off with whatever syrups, sauces, or jams you like, and dig in!

MAKES ABOUT A DOZEN 4-INCH PANCAKES

SMOKED CHICKEN

1¾ pound chicken
12 cups–1 gallon water
½ cup kosher salt
⅔ cup sugar
¼ cup olive oil
¼ cup hickory smoke flavor from concentrate
1 whole chicken, with innards removed

In a large container with a top, or in a brining bag, add the water, salt, sugar, olive oil, and hickory smoke. Stir well to combine, then gently submerge the chicken. Seal tightly and chill in the refrigerator for 4 to 8 hours.

Preheat the oven to 375°F.

Remove the chicken from the brine mixture and place on a roasting pan. Bake in the oven until the juice from the chicken runs clear and the internal temperature reaches 165°F, about 1½ to 2 hours. Remove from the oven and let cool. Remove the meat from the bones and shred. Store in the refrigerator until you're ready to use it.

SMOKED CHICKEN PANCAKES

1 package (12-14 ounces) pancake mix (choose your favorite)
1 cup loosely packed shredded or *diced* smoked chicken (page 12) for every 2 cups of pancake mix
2 tablespoons unsalted butter or canola oil. Can also use cooking spray.

Follow the instructions on the box of the pancake mix to make your desired amount of pancake batter. Stir the chicken into the batter until evenly distributed.

Heat the butter or oil in a large frying pan or griddle over medium heat. Use a ¼-cup measuring cup to create pancakes of your desired size in the pan or griddle. When bubbles form around the edges of the pancake, it's time to flip. Cook the other side until golden brown, about 1 minute. Serve warm with butter and syrup.

FUN FACT Pancakes are usually eaten on Shrove Tuesday as a way to use up any lard, sweets, and other food products that people give up for the Lent holidays before Easter. Shrove Tuesday, also known as Pancake Tuesday, Pancake Day, Mardi Gras, and Fat Tuesday, is the day before Ash Wednesday, and is celebrated all over the world. The celebration includes a pancake race where people have to run while flipping a pancake all the way to the finish line.

SPICY SAVORY GRILLED BREAKFAST

(GLUTEN-FREE IF USING GLUTEN-FREE BREAD)

There are mornings when the only thing that can start the day off right is bacon and potatoes with a kick. If you don't have time to sit at the table and enjoy this delicious sandwich, the recipe allows you to cook it up, spice it up, wrap it up, and eat it on-the-go. If you need something good and hearty to get you through most of the day, this could be the breakfast for you.

MAKES 1 SANDWICH

2 slices of bacon
¾ cup hash brown potatoes
1 tablespoon unsalted butter
2 slices sourdough bread
⅓ cup shredded cheddar cheese
Sriracha hot chili sauce, to taste

In a frying pan over medium heat, add the bacon and fry until crisp. Transfer to a paper-towel-lined plate. In the same pan, add the hash browns and cook until cooked through and golden brown. Transfer to a separate paper-towel-lined plate. Wipe the pan clean and add the butter. When this has melted, add the bread and cook until the slices are lightly golden brown on one side. Flip the slices over, and add your desired amount of shredded cheese to both slices. Place a lid over the pan and cook until the cheese is slightly melted. Add the hash browns and bacon to one of the slices; place the second slice on top, making a sandwich. Continue to cook both sides of the bread until each side is golden brown. Remove from the heat and serve with a side of Sriracha.

THE OFFICIAL CHASE 'N YUR FACE COOKBOOK

STUFFED HASH POTATO

(GLUTEN-FREE)

The basic, traditional hash brown is a popular and tasty side dish. But why settle for basic when you can have a jazzed-up, restaurant-style masterpiece made in your own kitchen? Peppers and bacon help bring the russet and sweet potatoes to life, and make this a great pairing with your morning eggs, or wrapped in a tortilla to take on the go.

Note: Before cooking your hash mixture, be sure to drain any excess water from your shredded potatoes. This will ensure that your hash crisps nicely. You can remove the water by wrapping small amounts of the shredded potatoes at a time in cheesecloth and squeezing.

SERVES 4–6

2 tablespoons canola oil
2 cups skinned, shredded, and rinsed sweet potatoes
2 cups skinned, shredded, and rinsed russet potatoes
1 cup diced bacon
¼ cup peeled and diced yellow onion
⅓ cup chopped red bell pepper
⅓ cup chopped green bell pepper
⅓ cup chopped yellow bell pepper
¼ teaspoon salt
¼ teaspoon black pepper

In a frying pan, heat the oil over medium heat. Add the shredded sweet and russet potatoes.

In a separate frying pan, add the bacon, onion, and bell peppers; cook over medium-high heat until the onions and peppers are soft, and the bacon is cooked, about 3 to 5 minutes. Remove the bacon, onion, and peppers from the heat and combine the mixture with the shredded potatoes. Continue cooking the hash mixture until it's golden brown. Season with salt and pepper.

FUN FACT African-American botanist and inventor George Washington Carver is probably best known for his peanut product inventions, but he invented over 118 sweet potato products as well. Some of Dr. Carver's sweet potato products include different flours, syrups, candies, breakfast foods, starches, wood fillers, and dyes.

SUNSHINE MUFFINS

I don't think you can have too many grab-and-go breakfast options. Ideally, we could all sit down and have a leisurely breakfast every morning, but for a lot of us that's just not possible. Bake these muffins the night before so they're ready for you to grab on your way out the door in the morning. Or be the one to surprise someone else with waking up to the heavenly smell of orange, cranberry, walnut, and spice baking in the oven. If you're not a nut person, feel free to hold the walnuts and just enjoy the fruit and spices. The flavors and aroma of these muffins will remind you of the holidays and put a smile on your face. They're also just enough to hold you over until your midmorning snack or lunchtime.

MAKES ABOUT 18 MUFFINS

2 cups flour
1 cup sugar
1 teaspoon baking soda
1 tablespoon ground allspice
1 teaspoon ground cinnamon
1 egg
¾ cup unsalted butter, softened
1 cup milk
2 tablespoons orange zest
2 tablespoons fresh orange juice
7 drops orange essential oil
1⅓ cups fresh or frozen cranberries

Preheat the oven to 400°F.

Line a muffin tin with cupcake liners (or use nonstick spray).

In a large mixing bowl, add the flour, sugar, baking soda, allspice, and cinnamon. Mix well to combine. Stir in the egg, butter, milk, orange zest, orange juice, essential oil, and cranberries.

Fill each muffin cup halfway with the mixture. Place the muffin tin in the oven and bake until a toothpick inserted into one of the muffins comes out clean, about 20 minutes.

FUN FACT The cranberry is one of the few fruits native to North America. Cranberries are grown mainly in Massachusetts, Wisconsin, New Jersey, Oregon, Washington, Quebec, and British Columbia. They're in the same family as blueberries, and are a good source of vitamin C. Because of this, sailors from America and Canada learned to take cranberries on long voyages to help prevent scurvy. And before that, Native Americans used them to make a food called pemmican a venison-and-cranberry mixture that could last a long time without spoiling.

SWEET FRENCH BREAKFAST

(GLUTEN-FREE IF USING GLUTEN-FREE BREAD)

Little did I know when I created this recipe that I'd be preparing it on *The Meredith Vieira Show*. Since Meredith's program aired during the morning-brunch hour, I decided this would be the perfect recipe for the occasion. Not only does my Sweet French Breakfast look and taste fantastic, but it reminds me of the amazing experience I had on her show. Have your own amazing experience when you treat yourself, your family, and guests to this favorite of mine.

SERVES 2

3 eggs
½ teaspoon ground cinnamon
2 teaspoons ground nutmeg
4 slices French brioche
2 tablespoons salted butter or cooking spray
3½ ounces Brie cheese
Powdered sugar or maple syrup, to taste
1 cup fresh berries (choose your favorite)

In a medium-sized mixing bowl, combine the eggs, cinnamon, and nutmeg. Heat a large frying pan over medium-low heat. Add 1 tablespoon of the butter to coat the pan.

Dip the brioche slices into the egg mixture, making sure both sides are coated. Add to the pan and cook one side until golden brown. Flip the bread slices over and add your desired amount of Brie on one of the

golden-brown sides of the bread, about 1½ ounces. Place a lid over the pan to allow the cheese to melt while the other side of the brioche bread turns golden brown, about 30 seconds to 1 minute. Remove the slices from the pan and place on a serving plate, stacking one on top of the other like a sandwich, allowing the cheese to continue melting. Keep warm while you repeat the process with the other two slices of bread. Sprinkle with powdered sugar or drizzle with syrup, if desired, and top with the berries. Serve warm.

FUN FACT

French toast isn't really French. Ancient Romans made this breakfast dish long before France existed. But technically, the Roman Empire controlled the land that later became France so Roman toast or French toast? Call it what you like!

VEGAN FIESTA BREAKFAST TACOS

This is a recipe for my vegan friends. And if you're one of those folks who think vegan food must be plain, tasteless, and boring, you'll be happy to discover you're completely wrong. These breakfast tacos are filled with spicy flavor, hearty textures, and all-around goodness. There's no way you can eat just one of these—you'll want at least two. If your carnivore friends insist, these tacos can be easily made with non-vegan products. But try this recipe first...I think you'll be pleasantly surprised.

MAKES ABOUT 10 TACOS

2 tablespoons canola oil or olive oil
¼ cup peeled and finely chopped shallots
½ cup chopped green bell pepper
½ cup chopped yellow bell pepper
1 package (14-ounces) vegan breakfast sausage
1 cup drained kidney beans
1 teaspoon Herbs de Provence
½ cup green chili enchilada sauce
½ teaspoon black pepper
10 corn tortillas
1½ cups shredded vegan cheese (provolone rice-based cheese works well with this dish)

In a pan, heat the oil over medium heat, and add the shallots, bell peppers, and breakfast sausage. Break up the sausage thoroughly so that it's the texture of ground beef, and cook the mixture until the peppers are soft. Stir in the kidney beans, herbes de Provence, green chili enchilada sauce, and black pepper. Reduce the heat to low and cook for an additional 10 minutes so the flavors can blend. Remove from the heat.

Scoop ¼ cup of the mixture into a warm or fried tortilla shell and top with shredded cheese.

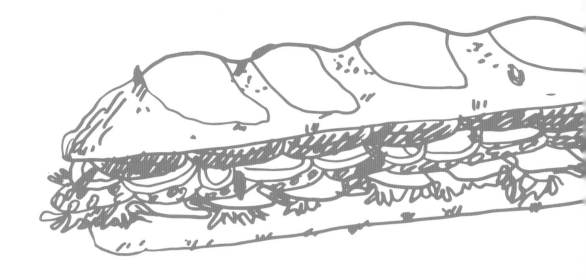

FEED THE BEAST

Depending on how my day is going, lunchtime is usually when I'm hungriest during the day. "Feed the Beast" is exactly how I feel! So I need foods that fill me up and refuel me without making me feel tired afterward. I also like having a variety of lunch choices throughout the week. One of the challenges I've faced is that I'm not into cold-cut, egg salad, PB&J, or tuna fish sandwiches—popular lunch food staples here in the United States. So I created my own lunch menu. And though I'm home for lunch on most days when I'm in town, these lunches are still suitable to pack for school, work, picnics, and short road trips. Salads, sandwiches, soups, and wraps are a few of the items you'll find on my lunch menu.

FUN FACT In the United States, lunch is usually a small or midsized meal and doesn't last longer than an hour. But in many other countries in Europe, the Middle East, and parts of Asia, lunch or luncheon is still the largest meal of the day, and many people will take two or three hours to eat and relax before continuing with their day. Employees and students often go home for lunch, and some businesses are even closed during lunchtime, including banks, government buildings, and university offices.

CAVEMAN KABOBS

(GLUTEN-FREE)

When I'm hangin' out with my bros, there's gotta be food and lots of it! These grilled kabobs are a great way to switch things up—fun and easy to make, crazy delicious, and healthy. You can always switch out different proteins, vegetables, and fruits to create your own flavor combinations.

SERVES 8

BEEF KABOBS

1½ pound Cubed beef (filet mignon or top sirloin)
1 tablespoon Texas chipotle BBQ seasoning (choose your favorite)
2 small Cubed Fuji apples (or choose your favorite variety)
1 small yellow sweet onion, peeled and cut into large pieces

CHICKEN KABOBS

1½ pound Cubed chicken pieces (preferably thigh meat)
1 tablespoon Rosemary Garlic Seasoning (choose your favorite)

1 mango, peeled and cut into large cubes
1 zucchini, cut into large pieces

CHICKEN BRINE

(OPTIONAL)

8 cups water
¼ cup salt
¼ cup soy sauce
⅓ cup olive oil
½ cup sugar

If you're using wooden skewers, soak them in water at least 1 hour before cooking.

In a large bowl, combine the beef and BBQ seasoning; let sit at room temperature for 1 hour. Meanwhile, cube the apples and peel and cut the onion.

In a separate large bowl, combine the chicken, rosemary and garlic salt; refrigerate until ready to use.

Note: If you prefer to add a little extra flavor, brine the chicken overnight using my brine recipe. Simply combine the water, salt, soy sauce, olive oil, and sugar in a large bowl, and add the chicken.

Peel and cut the mango and zucchini.

For each kabob, alternate the meat, fruit, and vegetables on each skewer, making sure to leave enough space between each ingredient.

Prepare an outdoor grill. When it's hot, place the skewers on the grill and cook the beef to your liking, and the chicken until it's cooked through.

FUN FACT

Kabob is also spelled kebab or kabab. In other parts of the world, the word describes all types of meats that are grilled, not just those on skewers.

FAMOUS KICK BACK PEPPER JACK

(GLUTEN-FREE IF USING GLUTEN-FREE BREAD)

When I was first starting to overcome my food aversions, cold deli meats were not something I was interested in trying. Then one day, I noticed the peppered roast beef at the deli. Long story short, I came up with this recipe as a way to introduce myself to a food that I wasn't sure I would like. I do like spicy foods, lots of different cheeses, and grilled cheese sandwiches, so I added the peppered beef to what I was already comfortable with. And yes, I was pleasantly surprised! I think you will be, too.

MAKES 1 SANDWICH

2 tablespoons salted butter
2 slices sourdough bread
4 slices thinly sliced Pepper Jack cheese
4 slices thinly sliced pepper beef deli meat

Heat a frying pan over medium heat.

Generously butter one side of each slice of bread. Place one slice of bread, butter-side down, in the pan. Layer the Pepper Jack cheese and pepper beef on the bread. Cook until golden brown, about 2 minutes.

Place the other slice of sourdough bread on top, butter-side up, and then flip the sandwich over and cook the other side until golden brown, about 2 to 3 minutes. Remove from the pan and serve.

FISH SUB

(GLUTEN-FREE IF USING GLUTEN-FREE BREAD)

When I was in London, I was honored to eat at some excellent Michelin-starred restaurants. But one of my favorite meals while I was over there was the traditional English fish-and-chips. Why? Because sometimes simple, fresh, tasty, familiar, and feeling part of the neighborhood is also a great dining experience. This recipe brings that experience back to me, and is another way to enjoy crispy, battered fish with a side of chips.

MAKES 2 SUB SANDWICHES

2 fresh sub rolls
Tartar Sauce (recipe follows)
4 breaded fish fillets (page 86)
Vegetable Slaw (recipe follows)

Open each sub roll and spread your desired amount of Tartar Sauce on both sides. Place two breaded fish fillets in the sub roll. Top with the Vegetable Slaw, and serve.

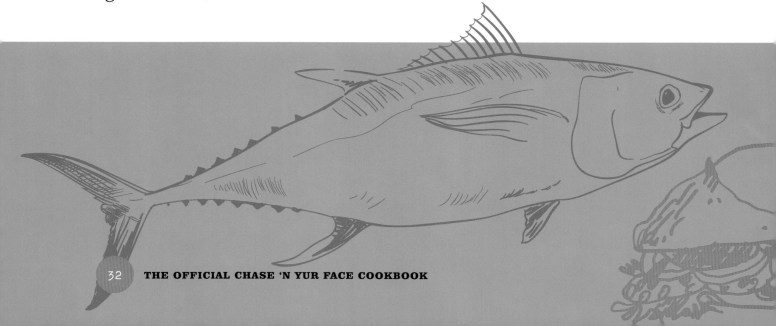

TARTAR SAUCE

MAKES 1 CUP

1 cup mayonnaise
2 tablespoons lemon juice
1 tablespoon sweet relish
1 tablespoon minced onion
Salt and black pepper, to taste

In a small mixing bowl, combine the mayonnaise, lemon juice, relish, and onion. Season with salt and pepper. Chill until you're ready to serve.

VEGETABLE SLAW

MAKES 1-1/4 CUP

½ cup shredded purple cabbage
¼ cup shredded carrots
½ cup shredded iceberg lettuce
2 tablespoon ginger-sesame dressing

In a bowl, combine the cabbage, carrots, iceberg lettuce, and ginger-sesame dressing. Chill until you're ready to serve.

FUN FACT Subs or submarine sandwiches are made on long bread rolls and filled with whatever kind of meats, cheeses, and/or veggies you like. The sub is named after its shape, which is like that of a submarine. But depending on where you're from, you may call this sandwich a zeppelin or zep, blimpie or blimp, grinder, foot-long, hero, po'boy, hoagie, wedge, or Gatsby. In New Orleans, Louisiana they make a sandwich called a muffuletta in which a round loaf or roll is used instead of elongated bread. But it's the same idea as the sub-shaped sandwiches. No matter what you call these, or if they're long or round, sub sandwiches are feasts designed to fill you up.

GRILLED CHICKEN PANINI

(GLUTEN-FREE IF USING GLUTEN-FREE BREAD)

You can cook the chicken on the stove or in the oven, but I recommend using an outdoor grill or barbecue. For me, grilling outdoors is such a relaxing and fun way to cook, and I love the way the food aromas fill the air. After you grill the chicken, the fresh mozzarella cheese, roasted red pepper, basil, butter, olive oil, and garlic turn this panini into a mouthwatering delight. This sandwich is perfect with a simple green salad and one of my refreshing fruit drinks.

SERVES 4

2 medium-sized boneless, skinless
chicken breasts
½ cup olive oil, divided
½ teaspoon salt
½ teaspoon black pepper
1 tablespoon fresh Italian parsley
3 cloves garlic, peeled and minced
8 thick (1-inch) slices French
bread, from loaf
3 tablespoons chopped fresh basil
4 large fire-roasted peppers
8 slices fresh mozzarella
¼ cup salted butter

FUN FACT
Thomas Edison invented the first commercial sandwich press, which we now call a panini press. But his invention wasn't popular with cooks, so it was discontinued in the 1930s. Fast-forward to 1970, when the appliance company Breville introduced their panini press. This time the world was ready for it, and the panini press has been popular ever since.

Place the chicken breasts in a bowl and add 1 tablespoon of the olive oil to coat. Sprinkle the salt, pepper, and parsley onto both sides of the chicken, and chill in the refrigerator for at least 30 minutes. Note: Pound the chicken with a kitchen mallet if the breasts are thick.

Prepare an outdoor grill or barbecue. When it's hot, add the chicken over direct heat, and grill until the juices run clear, about 10 to 12 minutes. Remove the chicken from the grill and slice.

In a small bowl, add the remaining olive oil and minced garlic. Using a pastry brush, lightly brush one side of each bread slice with the oil-and-garlic mixture. Sprinkle the chopped basil on top of the olive oil. Add the chicken, roasted peppers, and two slices of mozzarella. Close the sandwiches.

Heat a panini press to medium-high. Spread ½ tablespoon of butter on the outside of both sides of each sandwich. Place the sandwich in the panini press and cook until both sides are golden brown and the cheese is melted, about 3 minutes. Serve warm.

Note: If you don't have a panini press, heat a pan on medium heat and use a lid or a smaller pan as the press. Cook one side at a time.

HEARTY CHICKEN & LEMON VERBENA SOUP

When I visited the Culinary Institute of America–Greystone, one of the things I got to do was tour their amazing herb garden, where I got to sample fresh lemon verbena right off the plant. It was delicious! After that experience, I wanted to make my own dish that included fresh lemon verbena. I started by purchasing my own lemon verbena plant from a local nursery, then decided that I would use it in a soup. Now, let me say that I'm not a fan of most soups. I just don't like drinking a bowl of liquid with a spoon. But I thought using an ingredient that was new and interesting to me would help me create a soup I could get excited about—and it worked. Since I don't like watery soups, this recipe is on the thick and chunky side. And the flavors are mild and comforting, so people who are sensitive to spicier foods should really enjoy it.

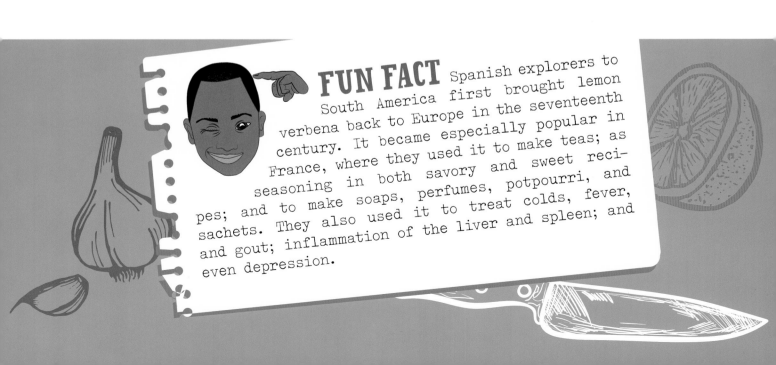

FUN FACT Spanish explorers to South America first brought lemon verbena back to Europe in the seventeenth century. It became especially popular in France, where they used it to make teas; as seasoning in both savory and sweet recipes; and to make soaps, perfumes, potpourri, and sachets. They also used it to treat colds, fever, and gout; inflammation of the liver and spleen; and even depression.

2 tablespoons olive oil

1 large onion, peeled and chopped

2 cloves garlic, peeled and minced

3 stalks celery, chopped

1 cup artichoke hearts

12 cups low-sodium chicken broth

2 tablespoons fresh lemon juice

3 cups shredded cooked chicken (Note: A fresh-cooked rotisserie chicken
    from the supermarket works great)

1½ cup wild rice, rinsed

1½ tablespoon salt

1 teaspoons black pepper

1 tablespoon chopped fresh Italian parsley

1½ tablespoons finely chopped lemon verbena leaves

2½ bay leaves

In a large slow cooker, add the olive oil, onion, garlic, celery, artichokes, chicken broth, lemon juice, chicken, rice, salt, pepper, parsley, lemon verbena, and bay leaves. Stir well and set to high. Cook for 6 to 7 hours.

MUSHROOM GRAVY SLIDERS

(GLUTEN-FREE IF USING GLUTEN-FREE BUNS AND
GLUTEN-FREE ALL-PURPOSE FLOUR IN THE GRAVY)

I've learned on my culinary journey that if I don't like a certain food item, it's usually because I don't care for the way the food is prepared. For instance, I wasn't a fan of the texture or taste of raw mushrooms, or having large mushroom slices on pizza. However, I discovered that I enjoy mushrooms when they are chopped in smaller pieces and added to gravy or sauces. I developed this recipe so I could include mushrooms (with all their nutritional benefits) in my diet. Having a variety of foods in my diet means I can get good nutrition from different sources, and helps me adapt to new foods when I travel. If you or someone you know has the same dislike for raw mushrooms, give this recipe a try. And if you already love mushrooms, this might become a new comfort food favorite for you.

MAKES 6 SLIDERS

¼ cup olive oil
1 cup diced portobello mushrooms
1 tablespoon minced garlic
¼ cup finely chopped shallots
½ teaspoon salt
½ teaspoon black pepper
¼ cup flour
¾ cup low-sodium beef broth
1½ cups milk
1 pound ground bison
6 slider buns

In a saucepan over medium heat, add the olive oil. When it's hot, add the mushrooms and sauté until soft, about 4 minutes. Add the garlic, shallots, salt, and pepper. Sauté for another 2 minutes, stirring occasionally. Stir in the flour and add the beef stock and milk. Continue to stir until the gravy has thickened.

Divide the ground bison into six equal pieces. Shape each piece into a patty.

Place the patties in a large frying pan and cook over medium heat to your desired doneness.

Assemble the sliders by slicing the buns in half and placing one patty inside, topped with your desired amount of mushroom gravy.

FUN FACT

Mushrooms are a type of fungus, and animals that eat fungi or people who hunt for edible wild mushrooms are called myco-phagists. In France, during the reign of King Louis XIV, people grew mushrooms in caves. This is because mushrooms don't have the green pigment found in most plants called chlorophyll, so they don't need sunlight to grow.

ORANGE WEDGE SALAD

(GLUTEN-FREE)

One of my favorite ways to eat fruits and vegetables is in salads with homemade dressings. Salads can make up an entire meal or just part of it. This recipe is crisp, refreshing, tangy, savory, and sweet. It's also easy to prepare, and has a cool-looking presentation.

SERVES 4

1 head iceberg lettuce
Blue Cheese Dressing, as needed (recipe follows)
½ cup dried cranberries
½ cup pine nuts
1 large orange, peeled and cut into bite-sized pieces
1–1½ tablespoons orange zest, for garnish
20 slices cucumber, for garnish

Cut the lettuce into four large pieces (wedges) and transfer onto four serving plates. Pour Blue Cheese Dressing over the top of each wedge. Sprinkle your desired amount of cranberries and pine nuts on top of the dressing. Add the orange pieces and a small amount of orange zest. Garnish each plate with slices of cucumber laid next to the wedge salad.

Blue Cheese Dressing
MAKES ABOUT 1¼ CUP
8 ounces fresh blue cheese, crumbled
¼ teaspoon kosher salt (optional; depends on saltiness of blue cheese)
¼ teaspoon black pepper
½ cup sour cream

½ cup buttermilk
1 teaspoon red wine vinegar
1 tablespoons fresh lemon juice
2 tablespoons finely chopped chives

In a small mixing bowl, add the blue cheese, salt, and pepper. Add the sour cream, buttermilk, vinegar, lemon juice, and chives. Stir well to combine.

FUN FACT

It is believed that oranges are native to Asia, and then were brought to Africa, the Middle East, and Europe. Christopher Columbus brought the first orange seeds to America around 1493. Now, oranges are found all over the world and used for many different things. For instance, orange oil from the blossoms is used to make flavorings and perfumes; oils from the rind are also used for flavorings; and oils from the leaves and stems are used in perfumes as well.

SALMON SALAD SANDWICH

(GLUTEN-FREE IF USING GLUTEN-FREE BREAD)

Sorry to say, I'm not a tuna guy. While others are chowing down on their tuna salad sandwiches, I'm savoring this Salmon Salad Sandwich on a fresh croissant roll because salmon is my favorite fish. You can use whichever bread you prefer, but I recommend croissants because their buttery, slightly sweet flavor complements the savory tastes in the salmon salad. Trying to help someone appreciate salmon? This is a great recipe to get them started.

SERVES 4

2 tablespoons olive oil
1 pound fresh wild-caught salmon fillet
¼ teaspoon salt, divided
⅛ teaspoon black pepper
¼ teaspoon chopped fresh parsley
½ cup low-fat sour cream
1 tablespoon fresh lemon juice
1 teaspoon dried dill weed
¼ teaspoon garlic powder
1 teaspoon sweet relish
1 tablespoon chopped green onions
1 teaspoon chopped chives
⅓ cup chopped celery
⅓ cup chopped water chestnuts
4 fresh croissants

Preheat the oven to 400°F.

In an 8 x 8 inch pan, add the olive oil and spread evenly on the bottom. Place the salmon, skin-side down, on the oil. Coat the top of the salmon using some of the olive oil from the pan. Season with half of the salt and the pepper, and add the parsley. Place in the oven and bake until cooked through, about 12 to 15 minutes. Remove from the oven and let cool.

Separate the salmon from the skin, and add the salmon to a large mixing bowl, breaking it apart with your fingers. Add the sour cream, lemon juice, dill weed, garlic powder, relish, onions, chives, celery, water chestnuts, and remaining salt. Stir until well combined. Serve on fresh croissants.

FUN FACT There is such a thing as "salmon candy." It's actually a sweet and salty smoked salmon jerky often made using salt, maple syrup, and brown sugar. Whether you're preparing salmon candy, smoked salmon rolls, or salmon fillet, it's always best to use wild salmon instead of farm-raised salmon, if you can. Wild salmon is firmer and has a lot less fat, with no chemical additives, which is healthier for our bodies.

VEGAN BLACK BEAN CHILI & SPICY CHEESY CORN BREAD

(GLUTEN-FREE)

Traditionally, chili has a brown-red color, with a tomato, beef, and pepper base. White bean chili is also popular. But black beans are my favorite bean, so I use them to make my meatless chili. I know that may sound weird, especially since I enjoy beef, but some things just are the way they are. With that in mind, I created this Vegan Black Bean Chili recipe. It's hearty, packed with flavor, and you can eat it as a side dish or as a main dish with tortilla chips or crackers. Top it off with sour cream or your favorite shredded cheese to give it a little something extra. And don't forget the corn bread! I've included my Spicy Cheesy Corn Bread recipe as well.

SERVES 8-10

1 bag (16 ounces) dry black beans
1 medium yellow onion, peeled and diced
2 cloves garlic, peeled and minced
½ teaspoon garlic powder
1 tablespoon salt
1–2 teaspoons red chili pepper flakes, or to taste
Tofu Mixture (recipe follows)
1 can (8 ounces) diced tomatoes
½ cup mild green chilies
2 teaspoons paprika
1 bay leaf

Rinse the black beans thoroughly, and add to a 6-quart slow cooker. Fill the slow cooker with water that comes 1 inch above the top of the beans and let soak for 5 hours. After soaking the beans, *keep the same soaking liquid,* stir in the onion, garlic, garlic powder, salt, and red chili pepper flakes. Then turn the slow cooker to high. Cook for 5 hours, stirring occasionally. After the beans are cooked, reduce the heat to low and stir in the Tofu Mixture, tomatoes, green chilies, paprika, and bay leaf. Cook on low for an additional 2 to 3 hours, stirring occasionally. Remove the bay leaf before serving.

FUN FACT The International Chili Society (ICS) was founded almost fifty years ago, and the first official Chili Cook-Off was held in Terlingua, Texas. No surprise, chili is considered the official state food of Texas, and it was a favorite of US President Lyndon B. Johnson—from Texas, of course. Today the ICS has grown to more than two thousand members with two hundred cook-offs every year in the United States, Canada, and Europe.

TOFU MIXTURE

1 package (8 ounces) extra-firm tofu

3 tablespoons olive oil

1 package taco seasoning (choose your favorite)

Remove the tofu from the package and press the water out by using a tofu press. If you don't have a tofu press, simply wrap the tofu in paper towels, place the wrapped tofu on a plate, and then add another plate on top of that. Add some weight (like a few cans from the pantry) on top of the plate and let sit until water is drained, about 1 to 3 hours.

Place the drained tofu in a mixing bowl and break it up until it resembles ground beef. Stir in the olive oil and taco seasoning, and refrigerate for 2 to 3 hours.

SPICY CHEESY CORN BREAD

MAKES 8–12 SLICES

Corn bread mix (8½ ounces; choose your favorite)

2 cups shredded sharp cheddar cheese, divided

¼ cup hot cherry peppers (for a mild flavor, use roasted green chili peppers)

Preheat the oven to the temperature indicated on the package of corn bread mix.

Spray a 9x5 loaf pan with nonstick spray or line it with parchment paper.

Prepare the corn bread batter according to the package instructions. Stir in 1½ cups of the cheese along with the peppers. Pour the mixture into the pan. Sprinkle the remaining ½ cup of cheese on top. Place in the oven and bake for the suggested amount of time. Remove from the oven and let cool before serving.

PICK-ME-UPS

Snacks can be anything from a small meal to a single piece of fruit or a few crackers. For me and most people I know, snacks have to be quick and easy to make and eat, so that we can get back to our daily work and activities. But that doesn't mean snacks have to be boring or junk food. Here you'll find recipes for dishes like a tangy tomato salad with Parmesan crisps, spicy hummus, a sweet panini sandwich, and a savory-sweet lettuce wrap with chicken and peaches, to name just a few. When you plan ahead and use great-tasting ingredients, snacks can be delicious, fun, and satisfying, and can make snack time one of your favorite times of the day.

FUN FACT A lot of us get hungry in the afternoon between three and four o'clock, and need a little fuel to get through our activities until dinner. So we have a snack. In Great Britain and other countries that were once a part of the British Empire, teatime usually falls between 4 and 6 p.m. No matter where we are in the world or what we call it, snack time is scheduled into our daily routines, and it should be nourishing and happen whenever our bodies really need it.

APRICOT AMAZEBALLS

Friends and family go wild for this recipe because it's flexible and unusual without being complicated. If you change just one ingredient, you can completely change the personality of the dish—add jalapeño to make it a side dish, or add sugar to the tempura batter to make it a dessert. Be adventurous and try it both ways. I think you'll be pleasantly surprised.

MAKES 10–15 BALLS

10–15 fresh whole apricots
10–15 pieces of mozzarella, the size of an apricot seed
½ jalapeño, diced (optional)
1 cup flour
1 tablespoon cornstarch
1½ cups seltzer water
1½ tablespoons sugar (only if making this recipe as a dessert)
1–1½ quarts canola oil

Slice the apricots in half and remove the large seeds. Place a piece of cheese in the center of one of the halved apricots. (Note: If you're making this as an appetizer, add the diced jalapeño to the cheese, if desired. If you're making it as a dessert, omit the jalapeño entirely.) Place the other apricot half on top.

In a medium-sized bowl, add the flour, cornstarch, and seltzer water, and mix until well combined. (Note: If you're making this as a dessert, add the sugar.)

In a large pot over high heat, add the canola oil. When the oil is hot, *approximately* 350°F., and working in batches, use a pair of kitchen tongs to dip the stuffed apricot into the batter and then transfer to the hot oil. Fry the stuffed apricots for 1 to 2 minutes, or until lightly golden.

Remove from the oil and transfer to a paper-towel-lined plate. Serve warm with a side of honey or Dijon mustard. As a dessert, serve with a scoop of vanilla ice cream.

FUN FACT

The apricot is a member of the rose family, and is considered one of the most nutritious, least fattening, and lowest-calorie fruits. In Chinese culture, apricots symbolize medicine, education, and health.

CHOCOLATE & PEANUT BUTTER BANANA BITES

(GLUTEN-FREE)

I created this super-simple recipe to go along with a product review I was invited to do for the Stivii Chocolate Variety Pack. Quick and tasty, these banana bites are an excellent alternative to sugary store-bought candies. They're also easy enough for even the youngest chefs in your house to make.

MAKES APPROXIMATELY 20 BITES MEDIUM SIZE

2 medium size bananas
2 bars (3½ ounces each) 56%-60% cacao dark chocolate.
2 tablespoons peanut butter

Line a 9 x 12 inch pan with parchment paper. Peel the bananas and cut them into ½-inch slices on the bias. Transfer to the parchment paper and arrange on a single layer.

In a small sauté pan over low heat, add the chocolate. Stir until melted. Stir in the peanut butter until well combined. Remove from the heat.

Using a spoon, drizzle the chocolate-peanut-butter mix over the top of the banana slices.

Place the pan into the freezer until the chocolate has set, about 15 minutes.

ENGLISH BRUSCHETTA

(GLUTEN-FREE IF USING GLUTEN-FREE BREAD)

I created this recipe for the 2015 British Asparagus Festival in Worcestershire, England, where I was invited to appear as a guest chef. I prepared this snack specifically for the kids attending the event. The bacon, honey, and cream cheese make these bites a hit with grown-ups, too. This is a wonderful recipe for introducing asparagus to those who haven't tried it yet.

MAKES 12–17 BITES

6–8 asparagus stalks, cut into bite-sized pieces
5 slices crispy bacon
1 baguette, cut into slices 1½–2 inches thick
1 package (8 ounces) cream cheese, softened
⅓ cup honey

Add the asparagus pieces to a steamer basket, over some boiling water, on medium-high heat. Cover and steam until the pieces are bright green and tender, but still somewhat crisp, about 6 to 8 minutes for thick stalks and 3 to 5 minutes for thin ones. Remove from the steamer and let cool. Meanwhile, fry the bacon until crisp, then finely chop.

Lightly spray a medium-sized frying pan with cooking spray and place over medium-low heat. Add the baguette slices and lightly toast both sides, about 1 to 2 minutes. Toast longer if you prefer crispier bread.

Remove the baguette slices from the pan and spread the cream cheese on one side of each. Top with the asparagus pieces and bacon bits. Finish with a drizzle of honey over the top.

HEIRLOOM TOMATO BASIL SALAD WITH PARMESAN CRISPS

(GLUTEN-FREE)

Okay, I'm just going to be honest here. I'm not a big fan of plain raw tomatoes, especially if they're swimming in seeds. Some people enjoy eating them like apples, or couldn't care less about the seeds. But that's just not me. On the other hand, if the seeds are removed and the tomato is chopped up nicely, like in a good Pico de Gallo (page 67), I'm cool with that. Now that I've gotten that out of the way, let me say that when it comes to eating fresh raw tomatoes, I think heirlooms are the best tasting and coolest looking. Their flavor and unique, colorful appearance really jazz-up this simple and refreshing recipe. You can dig into this salad and eat it like a dip with different chips, crackers, or breads that complement the flavors in the dressing.

1 cup grated fresh Parmigiano-Reggiano
3 large heirloom tomatoes, cut into bite-sized pieces
1/4 cup finely chopped fresh basil leaves
1 cup chopped cucumber
1/4 cup olive oil
1/4 cup apple cider vinegar
1 teaspoon salt
1/2 teaspoon black pepper

Preheat the oven to 350°F.

Line a baking sheet with parchment paper.

To make the Parmesan Crisps: Place 1 tablespoon of Parmigiano-Reggiano on the parchment paper. Using your fingers, spread the cheese into a thin, flat circular layer. Repeat, leaving about 1½ inches between each circle, until you've used all the cheese. Place in the oven and bake until the cheese is melted and slightly golden brown, 5 to 8 minutes. Remove the baking sheet from the oven and let it cool. Remove the crisps from the parchment paper using a spatula. Set aside.

In a medium-sized bowl, add the tomatoes, basil, and cucumber. Add the olive oil, vinegar, salt, and pepper. Toss well, and serve with the Parmesan Crisps.

FUN FACT The state fruit and state vegetable of Arkansas is the tomato. How could this be? Well, in 1893 the US Supreme Court ruled that the tomato is officially a vegetable. The Supreme Court decided that just as beans—which are actually legumes—are considered vegetables by people in everyday life, so too, are tomatoes. The Court went to the trouble of making it official because at the time vegetables were taxable, but fruits were not.

HUMMUS OF OLYMPUS

(GLUTEN-FREE)

Hummus is basically a dip made with cooked and mashed chickpeas, olive or sesame oil, lemon juice, and salt. It's delicious, healthy, and the kind of food that inspires me to be creative. I use my imagination and taste buds to add whatever ingredients I like—the sky's the limit for this snack. For this particular recipe, the gods of Olympus would be pleased because I incorporate Greek seasonings. Typically, hummus is spread on sandwiches, wraps, toast, and rolls. You can also mix it into meat dishes, or dip fruits, veggies, chips, crackers, fries, or cheese cubes into a bowl of it. The possibilities are endless. Low in fat and filled with protein, fiber, iron, magnesium, potassium, vitamin C, folate, and B_6, hummus is an outstanding alternative to junk food snacks. Try this recipe, and use your imagination to experiment with your own flavor combinations.

MAKES ABOUT 1 CUP

1 can (15 ounces) garbanzo beans
3 tablespoons olive oil
1 clove garlic, peeled and minced
2½ teaspoons Greek seasoning
1 teaspoon salt
1 tablespoon lemon juice
2 tablespoons warm water
1 tablespoon minced olives

Using a food processor, combine the garbanzo beans, olive oil, garlic, Greek seasoning, salt, lemon juice, and warm water. Mix on high until mixture is smooth, about 1 minute.

Scrape the mixture into a bowl and stir in the minced olives. Serve with pita bread, pita chips, or vegetables of your choice.

FUN FACT Hummus is the Arabic word for "chickpea," and chickpeas are also known as garbanzo beans. Hummus has been a food staple in the Mediterranean and Middle East for literally thousands of years. It is now so popular worldwide that filmmaker Oren Rosenfeld made a documentary film called *Hummus* that details the history of this food and depicts the ways hummus brings together people from around the globe. The film even features the *Guinness World Record* holder for the "Largest Serving of Hummus in the World," at 23,042 pounds. Now, that's a lot of hummus!

NACHO MI TACO

I created this recipe after filming with chef Gabbi Patrick at her restaurant, Gabbi's Mexican Kitchen. Her amazing signature seasonings and sauces got me thinking about how to get all the taco ingredients and flavors that I love on every chip—like a perfect nacho hors d'oeuvre plate. Don't get me wrong, a big pile of loaded, messy nachos is great, but there's a lot to be said for "the perfect bite." That's what this recipe is all about.

MAKES 16 LARGE NACHOS

3 tablespoons canola oil
4 large rice tortillas
15 ounces refried black beans
½ pound Nacho Mi Taco Slow Cooker Shredded Beef (recipe follows)
1 avocado, peeled, pitted, and sliced
½ cup sour cream
1 cup Pico de Gallo (recipe follows)

Preheat the oven to 350°F.

In a medium-sized frying pan over medium heat, add the canola oil. Cut the tortillas in half, then cut them in half again to make sixteen triangular pieces. Add the tortillas to the oil and fry on both sides until crispy, about 30 seconds to 1 minute. Remove from the oil and transfer to a cookie sheet. Spread some of the refried black beans on each piece. Add the shredded beef and the cheese. Place the cookie sheet in the oven and bake until the cheese is melted, about 7 to 8 minutes. Remove

from the oven and top each tortilla with a slice of avocado, a dollop of sour cream, and some Pico de Gallo.

NACHO MI TACO SLOW COOKER SHREDDED BEEF

[ADD YIELD HERE?]

1 tablespoon olive oil
3-pound boneless chuck (pot) roast
Nacho Mi Taco Slow Cooker Sauce (recipe follows)

Rub the olive oil on all sides of the roast. Place the pot roast in a slow cooker.

Pour the Nacho Mi Taco Slow Cooker Sauce on top, then cook on low heat for 8 to 9 hours, or high heat for 6 to 7 hours. Use a fork and knife to cut and pull apart the meat.

NACHO MI TACO SLOW COOKER SAUCE

MAKES ENOUGH TO SLOW COOK 1 3-POUND CHUCK ROAST

1 cup beef stock
3 tablespoons tomato paste
1½ teaspoons smoked paprika
2 teaspoons ground cumin
1 tablespoon chili powder
2 teaspoon salt
1 teaspoon garlic powder
½ teaspoon black pepper
½ teaspoon dried oregano
½ teaspoon onion powder

In a small bowl, combine the beef stock tomato paste, smoked paprika, cumin, chili powder, salt, garlic powder, pepper, oregano, and onion powder.

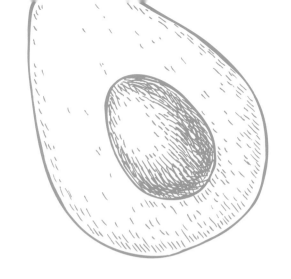

PICO DE GALLO
MAKES 4 CUPS

5 medium tomatoes, chopped

1 small white onion, peeled and chopped

2 jalapeños, seeded and finely chopped

¼ cup chopped fresh cilantro

¼ cup fresh lime juice

1½ teaspoons salt

In a small bowl, combine the tomatoes, onion, jalapeños, cilantro, lime juice, and salt.

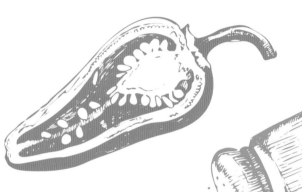

FUN FACT

In 1950, tortilla chips were introduced to the United States after a tortilla factory owner named Rebecca Carranza stopped throwing away the misshapen tortillas her factory couldn't sell. She simply cut the rejected tortillas, fried them to create chips, and sold them in her deli. Today tortilla chips are big business. They come in a variety of flavors and are one of the top-selling chip snacks.

PEACHY KEEN

(GLUTEN-FREE)

I think of this dish as a summertime lettuce wrap because it's refreshing and savory—but just a bit sweet as well. It also hits the spot anytime you're hungry, especially if you don't like anything too heavy on your stomach. This is a great recipe for people like me who have gluten sensitivities, or for those counting calories.

MAKES 8–10 WRAPS

1 cup diced or shredded cooked chicken breast (Note: A fresh-cooked rotisserie chicken from the supermarket works great)
½ cup grated sharp white cheddar cheese
3 tablespoons Poppy Seed Dressing (recipe follows)
8–10 leaves butter lettuce
2 tablespoons chopped almonds
1 ripe peach, pitted, and diced or cut into slices

In a small mixing bowl, combine the chicken, cheese, and Poppy Seed Dressing. Stir until well blended. Add approximately 2 tablespoons of this chicken mixture onto the center of a lettuce leaf. Sprinkle your desired amount of chopped almonds on top, and add a slice of peach. Repeat with the remaining lettuce leaves.

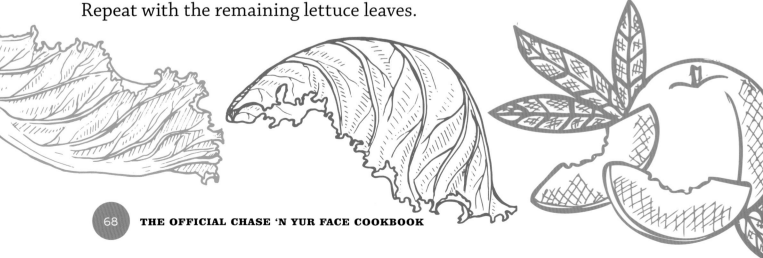

POPPY SEED DRESSING

(GLUTEN-FREE)

MAKES APPROXIMATELY 1½ CUPS

½ cup plain Greek yogurt
⅓ cup apple cider vinegar
⅓ cup canola oil
¼ cup granulated sugar
1 tablespoon onion powder
1 tablespoon poppy seeds
1 teaspoon gluten-free Dijon mustard
½ teaspoon salt

In a medium-sized bowl, add the yogurt, vinegar, oil, sugar, onion powder, poppy seeds, mustard, and salt. Whisk to combine. Refrigerate before serving.

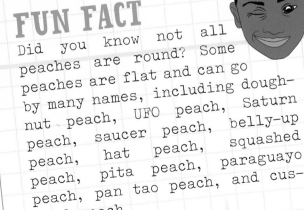

FUN FACT

Did you know not all peaches are round? Some peaches are flat and can go by many names, including doughnut peach, UFO peach, Saturn peach, saucer peach, belly-up peach, hat peach, squashed peach, pita peach, paraguayo peach, pan tao peach, and custard peach.

PEANUT BUTTER, NUTELLA, & APPLE (PBNA) PANINI

(GLUTEN-FREE IF USING GLUTEN-FREE BREAD)

Doing something different with a familiar dish or ingredient is what makes cooking fun and creative. Possibilities are endless and can change your mind about how, when, and where you eat something. For example, panini probably isn't something that jumps to mind when you're looking for a food to satisfy a sweet tooth. But after you try *this* panini recipe, it just might become one of the meals your sweet tooth craves—warm, gooey peanut butter, chocolaty Nutella, and apples all mixed together. Can you hear it calling your name?

1 small whole green apple
2 slices whole wheat sandwich bread (or gluten-free sandwich bread)
1 tablespoon Nutella
1 tablespoon peanut butter
Unsalted butter (optional)

Remove the skin from the apple with a peeler, then thinly slice the apple.

Spread the Nutella on one slice of the bread. Spread the peanut butter on the other. Arrange the apple slices on top of the peanut butter and top with the Nutella-spread bread slice.

Brush a small amount of butter on the top and bottom halves of the sandwich, or spray the top and bottom of a panini maker with cooking spray. Place the sandwich in the panini maker and cook until golden on both sides.

Note: If you don't have a panini maker, heat a pan on medium high heat and cook one side at a time using a lid or a smaller pan as the press.

FUN FACT The original Nutella recipe is the creation of Italian pastry chef Pietro Ferraro. Because chocolate was difficult to obtain during World War II and into the 1940s, Ferraro found that mixing a little cocoa into a hazelnut spread satisfied his customers' chocolate cravings while making the cocoa go farther during such lean times.

SPICY DOUBLE-DIPPED ONION STRAWS

MAKE GLUTEN FREE USING ALL PURPOSE
GLUTEN FREE FLOUR AND GLUTEN FREE PANKO.

Warning: If you're not careful, you *will* make an entire meal out of these extra-crunchy and spicy treats, munching your way to the bottom of the plate and then craving more. Fry up a few batches of these for your next at-home movie night or get-together.

SERVES 4-8

1–2 medium yellow or sweet onions
1¼ cups flour
1 teaspoon baking powder
1½ teaspoon salt + ½ teaspoon for
sprinkling after cooking
2 tablespoons taco seasoning
(choose your favorite)
Dash cayenne pepper
1 egg
1 cup milk
1 cup panko bread crumbs
4 cups canola oil
White cheddar cheese, grated,
as needed
Sour cream, for garnish
Chopped fresh cilantro, for garnish

Preheat the oven to 350°F.

FUN FACT

When you cut an onion, acids from the onion become a gas that is released into the air. When this gas comes in contact with the liquid in your eyes, it turns into sulfuric acid and burns. Fortunately, eyes produce tears to wash out this acid. Cooks who are sensitive to onions often use tricks like wearing goggles or freezing the onion before cutting. I like using a food processor—quick and tear-free.

Peel and slice the onions into ¼-inch rings and separate. Then cut the rings in half and set aside.

In a large bowl, combine the flour, baking powder, salt, taco seasoning, and cayenne. In another bowl, combine the egg and milk, and whisk together. In a shallow bowl or pan, add the panko bread crumbs.

In a large frying pan, heat the canola oil to 350°F.

Working in batches, coat the onion strips with the flour mixture, then dip into the egg mixture, and back into the flour mixture. Next, dip the onion strips into the panko bread crumbs until they're coated, and carefully place them into the hot oil. Cook until golden brown, about 1 to 2 minutes. Transfer the onion strips to a paper towel to soak up the excess oil.

Transfer the onion strips to a baking sheet pan lined with parchment paper. Sprinkle with salt to taste. Top with your desired amount of white cheddar cheese. Place in the oven until the cheese is melted, about 5 minutes.

Remove from the oven, transfer to a serving plate, and garnish with a dollop of sour cream and cilantro.

Spicy Double-Dipped Onion Straws can also be enjoyed with fresh homemade Pico de Gallo for dipping (page 67).

TROPICAL FROZEN YOGURT POPS

(GLUTEN FREE)

Fresh fruits and juices combined with yogurt make this a healthy, refreshing way to cool off and satisfy your sweet tooth. If you don't like strawberries or the other fruits in this recipe, select your own. Try different fruits, juices, and yogurt flavors to create unique frozen pops. Make a variety of flavors and invite your friends over to help taste-test on a summer afternoon when it's really too hot to do anything else except stay cool.

MAKES 8–10 ICE POPS

2 cups plain yogurt
2 cups chopped fresh fruit: bananas, oranges, and strawberries
½ cup powdered sugar
¼ cup fresh coconut water
¼ cup fresh pineapple juice

In a blender, add the yogurt, fresh fruit, powdered sugar, coconut water, and pineapple juice. Blend until smooth. Pour the mixture into ice-pop molds and freeze until frozen, about 5 to 6 hours.

LET'S FEAST

After a busy day of work, activities, and energizing meals, I think of dinner as a time to slow down, relax, and start enjoying the evening. On weekend evenings, I often have guests over for dinner so we can talk about what's new, laugh a lot, challenge one another to the latest video games, and just have a great time. Whether you're in the mood for meat or vegan dishes, or for something grilled, baked, fried, or slow-cooked, in this chapter you'll find recipes that are great for quiet nights at home or gatherings with family and friends.

FUN FACT

Do you know the difference between dinner and supper? Depending on your culture and where you live in the world, dinner can be a midday or early-evening meal. Supper is a lighter meal eaten after 8 p.m. For example, in Spain, a general daily meal schedule might be breakfast at 7 a.m., morning snack at 10 a.m., lunch from 1 to 3 p.m., dinner at 6 p.m., and supper after 9 p.m. (Lunch is the largest meal of the day; all the others are much lighter.) But whether you eat three, or five meals a day, and no matter if you call the last meal dinner or supper, make sure it's an easy, relaxing, satisfying feast for your senses that celebrates the end of another day.

BAKED TILAPIA & VEGGIE POTATO ALMIGHTY

(GLUTEN-FREE IF USING GLUTEN-FREE FLOUR IN THE GRAVY)

Tilapia is the perfect fish to go with my veggie potatoes with cheesy gravy. It's mild tasting and easily takes on the flavors of the other ingredients. Tilapia can also be enjoyed with a variety of foods including Mexican and Asian dishes. And the mild flavor makes it a good choice for introducing people to seafood.

SERVES 4

4 tilapia fillets
¼ cup olive oil
1 teaspoon salt
¼ teaspoon black pepper
1 teaspoon chopped fresh
Italian parsley
3 cloves garlic, peeled and minced
½ teaspoon fresh thyme
1 medium heirloom tomato, diced
2 teaspoons chopped fresh cilantro
Veggie Potato Almighty
(recipe follows)

FUN FACT

Tilapia is a warm-water, freshwater fish native to Africa and the Middle East. It has been a part of the Egyptian diet for over three thousand years. In ancient Egypt, people believed tilapia protected the sun god, Ra, on his journeys across the sky. They also used tilapia as a symbol of rebirth in their art, and the fish is associated with Hathor, Egyptian goddess of the sky, motherhood, love, beauty, joy, and music.

Preheat the oven to 350°F.

Place the fish in a baking dish and brush olive oil on both sides of the fillets, pouring any excess oil back onto the fillets evenly.

Sprinkle both sides with the salt, pepper, and parsley. On the top side of each fillet, add the minced garlic, thyme, tomato, and cilantro. Place in the oven and bake until the fish is cooked through, about 12 to 15 minutes. Remove from the oven, plate, and serve with Veggie Potato Almighty.

VEGGIE POTATO ALMIGHTY

For some of us, it can take a while to make friends with the veggie world. But once you do become friends, you'll find it's a world filled with amazing flavors and recipes that are also super healthy. This recipe is designed for those who need a little help getting themselves or someone they know into a veggie frame of mind. Veggies and potatoes are mashed, blended, and covered in a light cheesy gravy—all in all, a good way to get vegetable servings into kids' diets, while the adults will go back for seconds as well.

SERVES 6–8

5 medium-sized red potatoes, peeled
2 cups broccoli florets
3 cups cauliflower florets
2 cups medium-diced carrots
2 tablespoons unsalted butter
1/8 teaspoon salt
⅛ teaspoon black pepper

Fill a large pot half full with water. Add the potatoes and bring to a boil over medium-high heat. Boil the potatoes until they're soft, about 15 to 20 minutes. Remove the potatoes from the water and let them cool slightly.

Add the broccoli, cauliflower, and carrots to a steaming basket and place the basket on top of a pot filled with 1 inch of water. Cover with a lid and place over medium heat. Steam the vegetables for 10 to 12 minutes. Remove from the heat.

Add the potatoes, steamed vegetables, butter, salt, and pepper to a bowl. Using a potatoes masher, mash the ingredients together. You can use a hand mixer to help blend the ingredients, about 2 minutes. Serve with Cheesy Gravy over the top.

CHEESY GRAVY

MAKES ABOUT 3 CUPS

¼ cup olive oil
½ cup finely chopped onions
¼ cup flour
1 cup vegetable broth
2 cups milk
½ teaspoon salt
½ teaspoon fresh thyme
1 cup shredded Gruyère cheese

In a saucepan, heat the olive oil over medium heat. Add the onion and sauté until soft. Slowly stir in the flour. Add the broth and use a whisk to blend the mixture. Slowly stir in the milk and continue to stir until the sauce begins to thicken.

Add the salt, thyme, and cheese. Stir until combined. Remove from heat and serve with Veggie Potato Almighty.

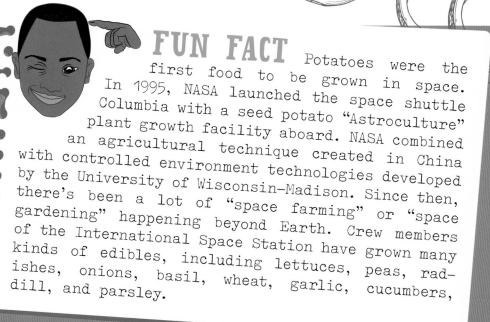

FUN FACT Potatoes were the first food to be grown in space. In 1995, NASA launched the space shuttle Columbia with a seed potato "Astroculture" plant growth facility aboard. NASA combined an agricultural technique created in China with controlled environment technologies developed by the University of Wisconsin–Madison. Since then, there's been a lot of "space farming" or "space gardening" happening beyond Earth. Crew members of the International Space Station have grown many kinds of edibles, including lettuces, peas, radishes, onions, basil, wheat, garlic, cucumbers, dill, and parsley.

CHICKEN AND VEGGIE VERDE ENCHILADAS

(GLUTEN-FREE IF USING GLUTEN-FREE CORN TORTILLAS)

It's important to eat your servings of vegetables every day. Wrapping them up in a tortilla with deliciously seasoned chicken and chili sauce makes veggies more of a treat than a have-to-'cause-it's-good-for-you kind of dish. The veggies in this recipe are those I enjoy in my enchiladas—I like the way they taste together. But there's no right or wrong combo to use. Choose whichever vegetables you like best.

MAKES 6–8 ENCHILADAS

1 tablespoon canola oil
1 medium yellow onion, peeled and julienned (optional)
1 medium red bell pepper, seeded and julienned
1 medium green bell pepper, seeded and julienned
½ teaspoon salt
½ teaspoon black pepper
3 cups fresh spinach
2 cups shredded cooked chicken breast (Note: A fresh-cooked rotisserie chicken from the supermarket works great)
1 (4-ounce) can green chilies
1 teaspoon garlic powder
½ cup sour cream
1 cup shredded mozzarella (can substitute Jack cheese), divided
6–8 flour tortillas
2½ cups salsa verde
1 (4-ounce) can sliced black olives

Preheat the oven to 350°F.

In a large frying pan over medium heat, add the canola oil. When the oil is hot, add the onions (if desired) and sauté until soft, about 3 minutes. Add the bell peppers, salt, and black pepper, and continue to sauté another 3 to 4 minutes. Add the spinach and sauté an additional 1 to 2 minutes. Remove from the heat and set aside.

In a medium-sized mixing bowl, combine the cooked chicken, green chilies, garlic powder, sour cream, and half the mozzarella cheese.

Spoon approximately ¼ cup of the shredded chicken mixture into the middle of each tortilla, and add your desired amount of sautéed vegetables. Roll each tortilla and place seam-side down in a 9 x 12 inch baking pan. Repeat with the remainder of the tortillas. Pour the salsa verde evenly over the top, followed by the olives and remaining mozzarella cheese. Cover with foil and bake until the cheese is melted and bubbly, about 20 to 25 minutes. Remove from the oven, and let sit 5 to 10 minutes before serving.

FUN FACT The word *enchilada* comes from the Spanish word *enchilar*, which means "to season, cover, or decorate with chili pepper," or "to add chili pepper." Wrapping a tortilla around other foods has been around since the time of the ancient Mayans.

FISH-AND-CHIPS

GLUTEN FREE IF USING ALL-PURPOSE GLUTEN FREE FLOUR

A lot of people use cod for traditional fish and chips, but I prefer halibut. It's mild, meaty, and versatile. It's perfect for batter-dipping, frying, and tastes great with these chips. Speaking of chips, I believe potatoes exist on this planet to be seasoned a million different ways, which is one of the reasons I like eating them, especially these chips. Instead of the traditional salt or vinegar, treat yourself and season them with parsley and lime. The chips are also fantastic with burgers, steaks, and fried chicken.

SERVES 4

THE FISH

MAKES 8- 2 OUNCE FISH FILLETS OR 16 - 1 OUNCE FILLETS

1 pound fresh halibut, skins and bones removed, cut into 4 equal strips
(you can also use other white fish, such as cod, haddock, or tilapia)
Salt and black pepper, to taste
1 cup flour
1 tablespoon cornstarch
2½ teaspoons dried dill weed
½ teaspoon baking soda
½ teaspoon salt
1 tablespoon apple-cider vinegar
2½ cups water
1 quart vegetable or canola oil

Season the fish with salt and pepper.

FUN FACT

In Britain, shops served fish-and-chips wrapped in newspaper until 1980, when it was decided that it was unsafe for the food to come in contact with newspaper ink. And in 1988, the first National Fish & Chips Awards were held in London.

In a medium-sized mixing bowl, combine the flour, cornstarch, dill weed, baking soda, salt, and vinegar. Slowly add the water and mix until smooth.

In a deep pan or wok, heat the oil to approximately 350°F, using a candy thermometer to check the temperature.

Dip the fish strips in the batter, coating all sides, and carefully place them in the hot oil. Fry until golden brown on all sides, about 2 minutes per side. Remove from the oil and drain on paper towels. Reserve and keep warm.

THE CHIPS
SERVES 4

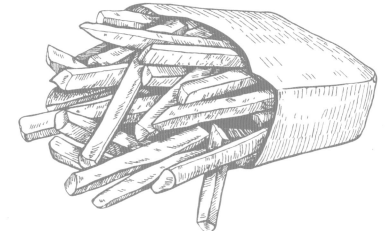

4 large russet potatoes
2 teaspoons salt
2 teaspoons black pepper
2 tablespoons parsley
4 lime halves

Rinse the potatoes thoroughly. If you prefer skinless chips, peel the potatoes using a potato peeler. Next, cut the potatoes in long strips like french fries. You can also use a food processor with the appropriate attachment. Soak the potatoes in water to cover for 30 minutes.

In a deep pan or wok, heat the oil to approximately 350°F, using a candy thermometer to check the temperature.

Remove the potatoes from the water and pat them dry with paper towels. Divide the fries into four batches. Line a cookie sheet or large pan with paper towels.

Carefully add the potatoes into the hot oil, frying one batch at a time until golden brown, about 5 minutes. Remove the chips and place on the paper towels to drain. Repeat with the other three batches.

Increase the heat of the oil to 400°F and fry the potatoes in batches again for 5 minutes. Remove the chips and set them on the paper towels to drain. Transfer the chips to a large bowl and toss with the salt, pepper, and parsley. Squeeze the juice from the lime halves evenly over the fries and toss again. Serve immediately with the fish.

GRILLED PORTOBELLO RICE BOWL

GLUTEN-FREE

One of the cool things about getting to meet and work with chef Roy Choi is that it made me want to learn more about Asian cuisine, and figure out ways to use Asian ingredients and flavors in my own cooking. In this simple, vegan rice bowl recipe, I incorporated BBQ teriyaki sauce and Asian five-spice powder (star anise, fennel seed, Szechuan pepper, cinnamon, and cloves), along with a little garlic and onion flavoring. This is a great dish for those times when you want a flavorful and filling meal, without the meat. The portobello, rice, and veggies make the dish hearty but still easy on the stomach, while the sauce and seasonings pull all the flavors together.

SERVES 4–5

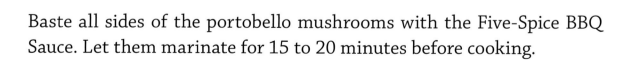

4 whole portobello mushrooms
Five-Spice BBQ Sauce (recipe follows)
4 bok choy, cut in quarters
1 cup daikon radishes sliced in rings
1 cup carrots sliced in rings
3 cups cooked jasmine rice

Baste all sides of the portobello mushrooms with the Five-Spice BBQ Sauce. Let them marinate for 15 to 20 minutes before cooking.

Grill both sides of the mushrooms on a prepared outdoor grill for 10 to 15 minutes using a low flame. Once they're cooked, remove the mushrooms from the heat and cut them into quarters. Baste with additional sauce, if desired.

Fill a pot that has a steamer basket with approximately 1 inch of water and set the basket inside. Place the bok choy, daikon, and carrots in the steamer basket and cover with the lid. Steam the vegetables over medium-high heat for approximately 7 minutes.

To serve, add the desired amount of rice in each serving bowl and top with the desired amount of vegetables and mushrooms.

FIVE-SPICE BBQ SAUCE
MAKES ABOUT 1/3 CUP

1/4 cup soy sauce
1/4 cup water
1 tablespoon Worcestershire sauce
2 teaspoons apple cider vinegar
2 teaspoons olive oil
2 tablespoons brown sugar
1/2 teaspoon five-spice powder
1/4 teaspoon garlic powder
1/4 teaspoon onion powder
2 teaspoons cornstarch

FUN FACT The word *teriyaki* actually refers to the method of grilling marinated meats. The sauce that we know today as teriyaki sauce can be traced back to Japanese immigrants who settled in the Hawaiian Islands. Teriyaki sauce is usually made with brown sugar, cornstarch, garlic, rice wine, soy sauce, and pineapple juice or a little cane sugar.

In a saucepan over medium-low heat, combine the soy sauce, water, Worcestershire, vinegar, olive oil, and brown sugar. Stir until the brown sugar has dissolved.

In a separate mixing bowl, combine the five-spice powder, garlic powder, onion powder, and cornstarch. Whisk the dry spices into the liquid mixture. Continue whisking until the mixture is smooth and thickens to the consistency of barbecue sauce. Remove from the heat and reserve until you're ready to use it.

JAMMIN' JERK ROAST

(GLUTEN-FREE)

The father of one of my best friends is from Jamaica, so I've been learning about Jamaican culture while enjoying authentic cuisine prepared at their home. In fact, I enjoy Jamaican food so much that it served as the inspiration for this recipe. Now, this isn't your traditional Sunday roast. The jerk spices and pineapple turn this roast into a jammin' party for your taste buds. And preparing the beef in a slow cooker leaves it so tender and juicy, it just falls apart. Serve this roast with rice and vegetables, make Caribbean tacos, or try it in sandwiches on toasted rolls.

SERVES 12–16

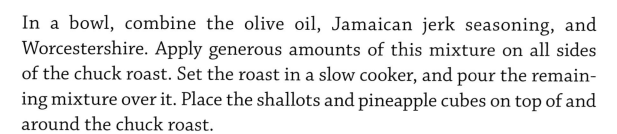

⅓ cup olive oil
2 tablespoons Jamaican jerk seasoning
¼ cup Worcestershire sauce
3½- to 4-pound chuck roast
2 tablespoons peeled and finely chopped shallots
20 pineapple cubes (about 1 inch)

In a bowl, combine the olive oil, Jamaican jerk seasoning, and Worcestershire. Apply generous amounts of this mixture on all sides of the chuck roast. Set the roast in a slow cooker, and pour the remaining mixture over it. Place the shallots and pineapple cubes on top of and around the chuck roast.

Set the slow cooker to high heat and cook until tender, about 5 to 6 hours.

MEXI-BURGERS

(GLUTEN-FREE IF USING GLUTEN-FREE BUNS)

This is the one that started it all—a taco on a burger! My very first recipe...feels like a million years ago. But it will always be a special favorite of mine, not just because it was the first one and has so many of my favorite flavors in it, but also because other people (including some I didn't even know) really liked it, and that encouraged and gave me the confidence to keep creating recipes. I guess I'm not the only one who enjoys eating a taco on a burger! Since then, I've made this for a couple of different casual events with family and friends, and there's *never* any leftovers.

SERVES 4

1 pound ground beef
1 package taco seasoning (choose your favorite)
1 cup sour cream
3 tablespoons spicy taco sauce
4 hamburger buns, toasted if desired
1 cup Guacamole (recipe follows)
4 slices cheddar cheese
1 cup Pico de Gallo (page 67)
1 cup shredded iceberg lettuce
16–20 nacho-flavored chips

In a large bowl, add the ground beef and mix in the taco seasoning. Divide the meat into four equal parts and form each into a patty. Prepare an outdoor grill or use a large frying pan over medium-high heat. Cook the patties to your desired doneness and set them aside.

In a separate bowl, add the sour cream and taco sauce; mix well to combine.

To assemble: Spread the guacamole on one side of each hamburger bun and spread the sour cream mixture on other side. Add the hamburger patty, cheddar cheese, Pico de Gallo, lettuce, and four or five nacho chips.

GUACAMOLE
MAKES ABOUT 11/2 CUPS OR 4 SERVINGS

2 medium-sized avocados, peeled and pitted
1 tablespoon finely chopped shallot
1 small tomato, chopped
¼ teaspoon garlic powder
½–1 teaspoon salt
1–2 tablespoons lime juice

In a bowl, mash up the avocados until they're creamy. Stir in the shallot, tomato, garlic, salt, and lime juice. Mix well to combine.

FUN FACT
Cumin, a main spice in taco seasoning, was sometimes used to pay taxes in the Middle East during ancient times. And during the Middle Ages, some people actually believed that cumin was a good-luck charm that would keep chickens and loved ones from running away!

PAPA BURGER

(GLUTEN-FREE IF USING GLUTEN-FREE BREAD
AND GLUTEN-FREE ALL-PURPOSE FLOUR)

My grandfather, Papa, was a serious burger lover like me. So you could say it's in my blood...*literally*. When my mom, aunts, and uncles were growing up, Papa would occasionally whip up his own restaurant-style burger using simple seasonings and ingredients, which he worked into the ground beef before he formed and cooked the patties. The patties were so delicious, you could eat them plain with a side of rice and a little gravy. Over the years, his patties and burgers have become legendary in our family. I asked Papa to teach me his recipe, and of course he did. You don't need to have exotic ingredients or a lot of items in a recipe for it to taste excellent—you just need the right ingredients, in the right amounts, and prepared properly. When you taste the Papa Burger, you'll know what I mean.

MAKES 4-6 BURGERS

1 pound ground bison or hamburger
1/3 cup chopped yellow onion
1 slice white or wheat bread, broken into pieces the size of bread crumbs
2 tablespoons red wine vinegar
2 tablespoons Worcestershire sauce
½ teaspoon garlic salt
½ teaspoon black pepper
1 tablespoon liquid smoke
1 teaspoon hamburger seasoning
¼ cup flour
Thousand Island dressing, as needed
4 onion hamburger buns, toasted if desired

1 large heirloom tomato, sliced
1 red onion, peeled and sliced
Butter lettuce, as needed

In a large mixing bowl, combine the ground meat, onion, bread crumbs, vinegar, Worcestershire, garlic salt, black pepper, liquid smoke, and steak seasoning salt. Use your hands to mix together thoroughly. Next, sprinkle some of the flour on a plastic cutting board. Form a patty with your hands (the patty doesn't need to be perfectly shaped). Press the patty on the board and lightly coat both sides with flour.

In a large frying pan over medium heat (or using an outdoor grill), cook the patties to your liking.

To assemble, spread Thousand Island dressing on each onion bun then add a patty along with tomato slices, onion slices, and butter lettuce leaves to taste.

FUN FACT Hamburgers have come a long way since the original Hamburg chopped steak patty, from Hamburg, Germany, was first put on a bun and turned into one of the world's most popular sandwiches. Hamburgers have evolved to include not just beef versions, but also venison, turkey, chicken, kangaroo, emu, crocodile, vegan, and even luxury "glam-burger" versions that feature foie gras, caviar, lobster, and edible 24 karat gold.

SLOPPY CHASE WITH LAMB

(GLUTEN-FREE IF USING GLUTEN-FREE BUNS)

A delicious lamb dish that I enjoyed at a local restaurant, served as the inspiration behind this recipe. Many people think serving lamb is reserved for a fancy dinner or special occasion. But I like to remind people that it can be an everyday food as well. Lamb is a meat that can handle strong seasonings. The key to this recipe is the spicy, rich sauce, which includes three kinds of peppers as well as a lot of garlic and onion. Top it off with fresh Parmigiano-Reggiano cheese and you have a sandwich fit for a king! Serve open-faced and eat it with a fork, or serve as a closed sandwich. Either way, I recommend a green salad with a creamy, Ranch Dressing as a light side dish.

SERVES 4-6

2 tablespoons olive oil
1 small yellow onion, peeled and chopped
1 tablespoon minced garlic
½ cup chopped yellow bell pepper
½ cup chopped orange bell pepper
¾ cup chopped cremini mushrooms
1 teaspoon salt
½ teaspoon black pepper
1 pound ground lamb
2 tablespoons Sloppy Joe seasoning
1 (6-ounce) can tomato paste
1 cup diced fire-roasted tomatoes with liquid
4-6 French brioche buns or regular hamburger buns
½ cup grated Parmigiano-Reggiano cheese

In a medium pan, heat the oil over medium-high heat. Add the onion and sauté 3 to 4 minutes. Add the garlic, bell peppers, mushrooms, salt, and black pepper; sauté an additional 2 minutes. Add the ground lamb and cook until the meat is cooked through. Remove from the heat and drain the excess grease, then return the mixture to the pan and stir in the Sloppy Joe seasoning, tomato paste, and roasted tomatoes. Put the pan back on the stove, reducing the heat to a simmer. Cover and let simmer for 30 minutes, stirring occasionally.

To assemble: Place ½ cup of the mixture on one side of each bun and sprinkle with cheese. Top with the other half of the bun. To make an open-faced sandwich, place ½ cup of the mixture on each half of the bun and sprinkle with cheese. Serve warm.

FUN FACT This type of sandwich is known by many different names. Depending on where you're from, you may call it a Loose Meat Sandwich, Chopped Meat Sandwich, Sloppy Joe, Dynamite Sandwich, Hamburg à la Creole, Rou Jia Mo, Keema Pav, or Spanish-Style Minced Beef Sandwich, to name a few of its monikers. The meats, sauce ingredients, seasonings, and breads vary from sandwich to sandwich, but the concept remains the same: meat in sauce on bread.

STRONG & SPICY BURGERS

(GLUTEN-FREE IF USING GLUTEN-FREE BUNS)

This recipe uses Sriracha and aioli to turn up the heat and spice. If a burger with attitude is what you're after, then the Strong & Spicy Burger is the one for you. I highly recommend that you enjoy this with one of the refreshing drinks in the Cool Breezes section of this book.

1½ pounds ground beef
Salt and black pepper, to taste
¾ cup crumbled blue cheese
8 slices bacon
1 tablespoon olive oil
1 small yellow onion, peeled and
sliced into rings
24 ounces fresh spinach
½ cup Sriracha Aioli (recipe follows)
4 brioche hamburger buns, toasted if desired

Divide the ground beef into four equal parts, and form each into a hamburger patty. Season with salt and pepper.

In a large frying pan over medium heat, or on a prepared outdoor grill, add the patties and cook to your desired doneness. Just before removing them from the heat, add the blue cheese and let it melt slightly.

In a separate pan, or on the grill, cook the bacon. Remove from the heat and set aside to drain on paper towels.

In a pan, heat the olive oil over medium-high heat. Add the onion and sauté about 4 minutes. Add the spinach and sauté until wilted, about 1 to 2 minutes. Remove from the heat.

Assemble the hamburger by adding the Sriracha Aioli to both sides of each hamburger bun. Add the burger topped with blue cheese, then the sautéed onions and spinach; finish with two slices of bacon.

SRIRACHA AIOLI

MAKES ABOUT 1 CUP

1 cup mayonnaise

1½ tablespoons Sriracha hot chili sauce

1 teaspoon garlic paste

¼ teaspoon salt

¼ teaspoon black pepper

In a medium-sized mixing bowl, add the mayonnaise, Sriracha, garlic paste, salt, and pepper. Mix until well combined with a smooth consistency. Refrigerate until you're ready to serve.

FUN FACT Sriracha is named for the town of Sri Racha, Thailand, where the sauce originally came from. There are lots of sauces that call themselves Sriracha, but the popular Sriracha HOT Chili Sauce with the rooster logo, green cap, and writing in five languages on the label comes from David Tran, founder of Huy Fong Foods in Southern California. David Tran and his family came to the United States from South Vietnam in 1980, and he started his business making the sauce by hand in buckets, and selling it to local restaurants. Now it's a multimillion-dollar enterprise.

TIKKA MASALA PIZZA

(GLUTEN-FREE IF USING GLUTEN-FREE PIZZA DOUGH)

To me, some of the most delicious and authentic foods are fusion dishes, which combine cuisines from different cultures. This recipe combines Italian, Indian, and British influences to create a simple, familiar dish that's still new and fun for your taste buds.

MAKES 4–6 PIZZAS

¼ cup olive oil
¾ cup chopped yellow onions
1 cup diced cremini mushrooms
3 cloves garlic, peeled and minced
2 teaspoons ground turmeric
1 tablespoon paprika
1 tablespoon coriander seed powder
2 teaspoons ground cumin
1 teaspoon salt
¼ teaspoon ground cardamom seed
½ teaspoon dried tarragon
8 ounces tomato sauce
1 cup roasted tomatoes
½ cup vegetable broth
2 tablespoons lemon juice
4-6 Naan Bread
2 cups shredded goat mozzarella cheese

In a saucepan over medium heat, add the olive oil, onions, and mushrooms. Sauté for about 4 minutes. Add the garlic and sauté another 2

minutes. Add the turmeric, paprika, coriander, cumin, salt, cardamom, and tarragon. Stir continuously until well blended, about 1 minute. Stir in the tomato sauce, roasted tomatoes, broth, and lemon juice. Reduce the heat to low and simmer for 30 minutes, stirring occasionally.

Preheat the oven to 350°F.

Place the naan bread on a pizza round or cookie sheet. Spread approximately ¼ cup of the tikka masala sauce on the bread. Top with your desired amount of cheese. Place in the oven and bake until the cheese is melted and golden brown, about 10 to 12 minutes.

FUN FACT Tikka masala originated not in India, as many people presume, but in Indian restaurants in Great Britain during the 1960s to please the taste buds of native Brits. Over the years, the dish has become so popular in Britain that many people consider it their national dish. Along with traditional foods like fish-and-chips, bangers and mash, and shepherd's pie, tikka masala can be found on menus in pubs and restaurants all across Britain. Originally it consisted of chicken pieces, but vegetables and other meats now find their way into the sauce.

VEGGIE-GHETTI

(GLUTEN-FREE)

California Bountiful honored me with my first magazine cover feature. To celebrate the occasion and pay tribute to California farmers and their outstanding produce, I created a veggie, gluten-free pasta dish. It's also a great recipe to help kids eat, enjoy, and try new vegetables.

SERVES 4–6

1 (8- to 12-ounce) package gluten-free spaghetti
½ cup olive oil
½ cup chopped green zucchini
½ cup chopped yellow zucchini
½ cup chopped orange bell pepper
5–6 cloves garlic, peeled and finely chopped
2 medium-sized tomatoes, chopped
½ teaspoon salt
½ teaspoon black pepper
2 cups fresh spinach leaves
1 cup shredded Parmesan cheese

Cook the spaghetti according to the package directions, and drain. Set aside.

In a large saucepan, heat the oil over medium heat. Add the zucchini and bell pepper, and sauté for 2 to 3 minutes. Add the garlic, tomatoes, salt, and pepper, and sauté an additional 2 minutes. Slowly stir in the spaghetti and spinach, making sure all the ingredients are well blended. Divide onto individual serving plates and serve immediately with Parmesan cheese sprinkled over the top.

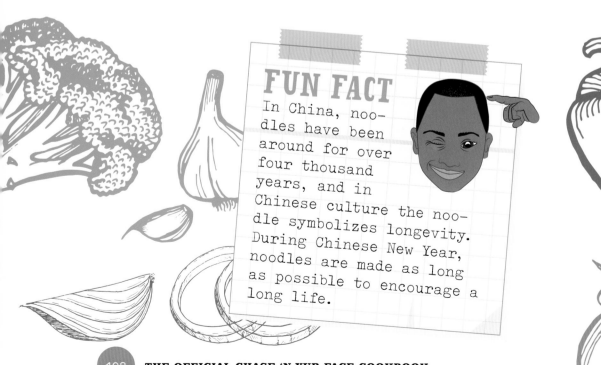

FUN FACT

In China, noodles have been around for over four thousand years, and in Chinese culture the noodle symbolizes longevity. During Chinese New Year, noodles are made as long as possible to encourage a long life.

LIFE IS SWEET

To me, desserts are a kind of "soul-food." Do our bodies need them to survive? No, of course not. But we are more than just bodies, and I believe we need things that make our souls happy and literally make life sweet. However, too many desserts is not a good thing, and I totally get that some people have to be more careful than others about eating sweets – I'm one of those people. But a little sweet now and then is the bonus that turns a good meal into a party. So whether you like your desserts fruity, chocolatey, spicy, buttery, or salty-sweet, I'm sure you'll find dessert recipes here that will make your life sweeter.

FUN FACT

Desserts weren't always the kind of creations that we are familiar with today. In ancient times, desserts were nuts and fruits rolled in honey. As skills, tools, and technology got better, and people traveled to other lands and discovered new foods, herbs, and spices, making desserts became more interesting. It's also interesting to note that some of the items we think of as sweets—like chocolate, ginger, lemon, licorice, and rhubarb—were actually first used as medicines. Those are my kind of medicines!

BANANA SPLIT MINI MOIST CAKES

After I was a featured guest in GE Appliances *Our American Kitchen* series, GE asked me to create a recipe to show how well their GE Profile Series Over-the-Range Oven with Advantium Technology could bake. The results were a win–win. The oven did an excellent job and the recipe scored big points with those who tried it. This recipe also makes dessert taste and look like a celebration.

MAKES 12-16 MINI CAKES

1 16 ounce package Chocolate cake box mix
½ cup unsalted butter (to substitute for the oil in the cake mix recipe)
2 cups ripe mashed banana
2 egg yolks
½ teaspoon baking soda
1 3½ ounce package banana pudding
Whipped cream, as needed, for garnish
Chocolate syrup, as needed, for garnish
Finely chopped walnuts, as needed, for garnish
12 maraschino cherries, for garnish

Preheat the oven to 350°F.

Follow the directions on the cake mix box to make a batter, but substitute butter for the oil.

In a separate bowl, follow the directions on the banana pudding box to make the pudding.

Stir the bananas, egg yolks, and pudding into the cake box mix until well blended. Next, stir in the baking soda. Using an electric mixer set to medium speed, mix the batter until well blended.

Use cooking spray to lightly grease a muffin tin. Scoop the cake batter into the muffin cups, filling each three-quarters of the way full. Place in the oven and bake until a toothpick inserted into the mini cakes comes out clean, about 20 minutes. Remove from the oven and let cool.

Note: When the mini cakes are baking, you will see them rise like a cupcake, but when you remove them from the oven, the tops will begin to settle into a slight indentation. The tops will also be moist. This is how you want them to look and feel.

When the mini cakes are cool, top each with a dollop of whipped cream, a drizzle of chocolate syrup, some finely chopped walnuts, and a cherry.

FUN FACT
In 1904, David Evans Strickler, who worked at a pharmacy in Latrobe, Pennsylvania, invented the banana split. Back then it cost only ten cents!

BROWNIE S'MORES SANDWICHES

(GLUTEN-FREE IF USING GLUTEN-FREE BROWNIE MIX, MARSHMALLOW FLUFF, AND GRAHAM CRACKERS)

Hmmm...Which do I want for dessert...brownies or s'mores? Why do I have to choose just one or the other? Why not have *both* of them in one out-of-this-world recipe! That is how my Brownie S'mores Sandwich was born; and the rest, as they say, is history. This is a real party pleaser.

MAKES 9–12 SANDWICHES

1 16 ounce package brownie mix (choose your favorite)
1 (7-ounce) jar marshmallow fluff
5 full-sized graham crackers

Preheat the oven to the temperature indicated on the package of brownie mix.

Line two 9 x 5 inch loaf pans with parchment paper (or spray with non-stick spray).

Prepare the brownie mix batter according to the package instructions. Pour ½ of the brownie mix into each of the pans and spread evenly. Bake at the suggested temperature and for the suggested length of time. Remove from the oven and let cool.

Remove both brownies from the pan by first removing the parchment paper, then flipping the brownies carefully onto a large cutting board.

Using a microwavable container, warm the marshmallow fluff for about 15 seconds. Do not overheat. The marshmallow fluff should just be warm and easy to spread.

Using a frosting spatula or knife, spread half of the marshmallow fluff on the top of one brownie and spread the other half on the second, making sure to cover the entire surface of each brownie.

Place the graham crackers side by side on top of one of the marshmallow-covered brownies. Take the second brownie, with the marshmallow side facing down, and place it on top of the graham crackers. Cut into your desired number of pieces and serve with milk or ice cream.

FUN FACT S'mores have been around since the 1920s and were made popular by the Boy and Girl Scouts for camping trips. But before that, cookies, marshmallows, and chocolate were being eaten together in Mallomars since 1913 and in MoonPies since 1917.

COCA-COLA CAKE

This is another Bailey family favorite that I heard a lot about from my mom, aunts, and uncles. My great-grandmother Finley made a Coca-Cola Cake on special occasions. I took her recipe and kicked it up a notch using more chocolate, more butter, and a few little changes in the rest of the ingredients. The result is a cake that is completely addicting in a *really* good way. I haven't met a chocoholic who hasn't gone nuts for this recipe once they've tried it. It's not the fanciest-looking chocolate cake you'll see, and you can forget about counting calories. This one is all about taste, happiness, and comfort.

MAKES 1 CAKE, ABOUT 18 SLICES

2 sticks (1 cup) unsalted butter
1 square (1 ounce) semisweet baking chocolate
1 cup cola
¾ cup miniature marshmallows
½ cup vegetable oil
2 teaspoons vanilla extract
2 cups sugar
2 eggs
¾ cup buttermilk
2⅓ cups all-purpose flour
¾ cup cocoa powder
1½ teaspoons baking powder
1 teaspoon baking soda
½ teaspoon salt

Preheat the oven to 350°F.

Spray a 9 x 13 inch cake pan with cooking spray.

In a medium size pot over medium heat, melt the butter and semisweet baking chocolate, stirring often. Add the cola and bring to a boil. As soon as the mixture is boiling, immediately remove it from the heat and add the marshmallows. Stir until well blended, then set aside to cool.

In a large mixing bowl, add the vegetable oil, vanilla, sugar, eggs, and buttermilk. Beat with a mixer until smooth.

In a separate medium-sized mixing bowl, combine the flour, cocoa powder, baking powder, baking soda, and salt.

Pour half of the flour mixture into the bowl with the liquid ingredients and blend. Then add the cooled cola mixture to the bowl, and beat with a mixer until well incorporated.

Pour the remainder of the flour mixture into the bowl and beat for about 2 to 3 minutes.

Pour the batter into the cake pan, and bake in the oven until a toothpick inserted into the cake comes out clean, about 35 to 40 minutes. Remove and let cool. Frost the top of the cake and serve.

FROSTING
MAKES ABOUT 2 CUPS

3 sticks (1½ cups) softened unsalted butter
4 cups powdered sugar
¾ cup cocoa powder
1 teaspoon vanilla extract

1 tablespoon chocolate syrup

3 tablespoons cola

In a large mixing bowl, add the butter, sugar, cocoa powder, vanilla, chocolate syrup, and cola. Beat with a mixer until smooth. Note: Add more cola if you want the frosting thinner.

FUN FACT

For the 1971 film Willy Wonka & the Chocolate Factory, the filmmakers created an actual chocolate river for the famous scene of Augustus Gloop almost drowning! They used 15,000 gallons of water mixed with chocolate and cream. Swimming in chocolate may sound like fun, but the cream spoiled really quickly, which of course, made the set smell horrible!

FESTIVE PRETZEL SALAD

(GLUTEN-FREE IF USING GLUTEN-FREE PRETZELS AND GRANOLA)

The basic Pretzel Salad has been around for a while, and is one of my mom's all-time favorites. She loves strawberries, and the combinations of salty-sweet and creamy-crunchy. For fun, I decided to give the recipe a makeover with a few changes and added ingredients. I think you'll enjoy the party of flavors and textures dancing around in your mouth. The other fun thing about this recipe is that it's called a "salad," even though we all know it's a dessert. But it always sounds better to say, "I had a salad for dessert" than "I had dessert for lunch," right? (Come on now...admit it...we've all had dessert for lunch at one time or another.)

SERVES 12-16

1½ cups crushed pretzels
1 cup honey almond granola
¾ cup melted unsalted butter
2 tablespoons brown sugar
1 (6-ounce) package raspberry gelatin
½ cup fresh blueberries
½ cup halved fresh blackberries
1 cup fresh strawberries, sliced
1 (8-ounce) package cream cheese
1 (8-ounce) container whipped topping
½ cup sugar
1 banana

Preheat the oven to 400°F.

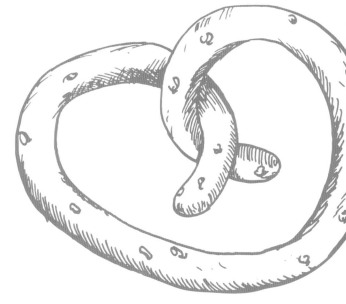

In a medium-sized mixing bowl, combine the crushed pretzels, granola, butter, and brown sugar. Spread the pretzel mixture evenly on the bottom of a 9 x 13 inch pan. Place in the oven and bake for 8 to 10 minutes. Remove from the oven and let cool.

In a separate mixing bowl, follow the instructions on the raspberry gelatin package, adding the fresh fruit to the liquid gelatin. Then place the gelatin in the refrigerator until the liquid is slightly gelled (it should resemble the consistency of scrambled eggs), about 3 hours.

Using a hand mixer in another mixing bowl, blend the cream cheese, whipped topping, sugar, and banana until smooth.

Spread the cream cheese mixture evenly on top of the pretzel-and-granola mixture, making sure to seal all corners of the pan. Pour the gelatin on top of the cream cheese layer. Refrigerate until set, about 2 hours.

FUN FACT Jell-O, one of the ingredients in this recipe, has been around since the early 1900s. It originally came in four fruit flavors (Strawberry, Raspberry, Lemon, and Orange), but over the years more flavors were added, including some savory ones that didn't catch on, like Celery, Italian Salad, Mixed Vegetable, and Seasoned Tomato.

GRANDMA KAREN'S GINGERBREAD

I never got to meet Grandma Karen, but my mom, aunts, and uncles have many fond memories of her. And one of those memories is enjoying her homemade gingerbread during the autumn and winter holiday seasons. When I received the recipe and tried it, I understood why—warm, spicy goodness that goes perfectly with whipped cream, vanilla ice cream, eggnog, teas, coffees, a glass of milk, or just by itself. It also makes the entire house smell amazing.

MAKES ABOUT 8 SLICES

1½ cups all-purpose flour
1 teaspoon ground ginger
1 teaspoon ground cinnamon
¾ teaspoon baking powder
½ teaspoon baking soda
½ teaspoon salt
½ cup soft unsalted butter
¼ cup dark brown sugar
1 egg
½ cup dark molasses
½ cup boiling water

Preheat the oven to 350°F.

Spray a 9 x 5 x 3 inch loaf pan or 9 x 9 x 2 inch baking pan with cooking spray. Then dust the interior with flour.

In a large mixing bowl, combine the flour, ginger, cinnamon, baking powder, baking soda, and salt.

In a separate large mixing bowl, use a spoon to combine the butter, brown sugar, egg, and molasses. Then use a hand or electric mixer and beat for 1 minute.

Pour half of the dry ingredients and all of the water into the bowl with the wet ingredients, and beat for about 30 seconds. Then pour in the remaining dry ingredients and beat for another 30 seconds. Pour the batter into the pan and bake in the oven until a toothpick inserted into the cake comes out clean, about 30 to 35 minutes. Remove and let cool for about 10 minutes. Remove from the pan and serve warm.

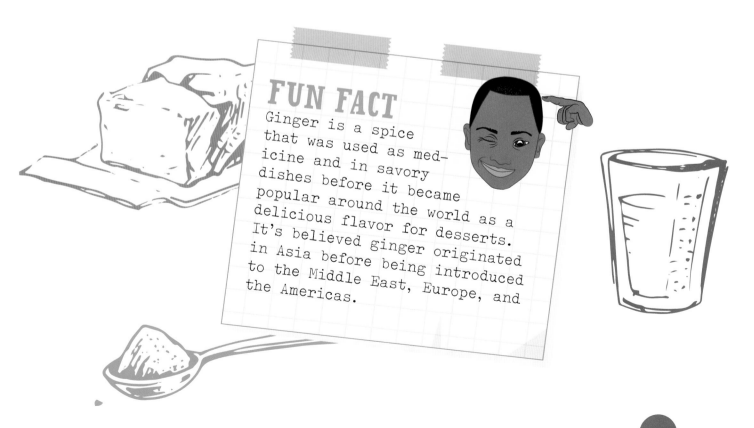

FUN FACT
Ginger is a spice that was used as medicine and in savory dishes before it became popular around the world as a delicious flavor for desserts. It's believed ginger originated in Asia before being introduced to the Middle East, Europe, and the Americas.

LEMONADER

I developed this recipe after being invited to do a product review for a nonstick brownie pan. As crazy as I am about chocolate, there are other flavors that my sweet tooth longs for, so I used this as an opportunity to whip-up a recipe to satisfy my lemon and raspberry cravings. With a scoop of vanilla ice cream, this simple and flavorful dessert is a delicious way to top off a meal.

MAKES 1 CAKE

Lemon Cake
¾ cup flour
¾ cup granulated sugar
¼ teaspoon salt
½ cup soft salted butter
2 large eggs
2 tablespoons fresh lemon zest
2 tablespoons lemon juice
Raspberry Syrup (recipe follows)

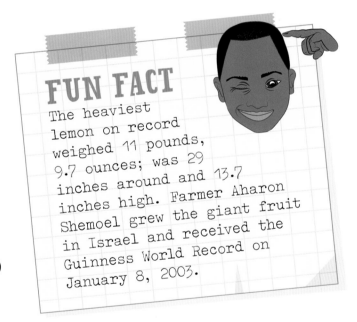

FUN FACT
The heaviest lemon on record weighed 11 pounds, 9.7 ounces; was 29 inches around and 13.7 inches high. Farmer Aharon Shemoel grew the giant fruit in Israel and received the Guinness World Record on January 8, 2003.

Preheat the oven to 350°F.

In a medium-sized mixing bowl, combine the flour, sugar, salt, and butter.

In a small mixing bowl, whisk together the eggs, lemon zest, and lemon juice. Fold the egg mixture into the flour mixture.

Spray an 8 x 8 inch pan (or brownie pan) with cooking spray. Pour the mixture into the pan. Place in the oven and bake until a toothpick inserted into the cake comes out clean, about 20 minutes. Remove from the oven and let cool. Cut into slices and top with raspberry syrup.

RASPBERRY SYRUP
MAKES ABOUT 1-1/2 CUPS

1½ cups frozen raspberries (defrosted)
1 cup powdered sugar

Defrost the raspberries. Mix the raspberries and powdered sugar in a blender until well combined.

NOT YOUR AVERAGE OATMEAL COOKIE

I really wanted to make a big, soft, chewy cookie that combined favorite flavors with a little bit of a twist. People are familiar with lemon and blueberry, but many have still not tried lavender in their food, or don't recognize the taste when they eat it, or haven't thought about how it can be used to make an ordinary recipe taste new. So I included lavender in these cookies to get people comfortable with the taste. And guess what? People are loving it!

12-18 COOKIES

1 cup sugar
½ cup packed brown sugar
2 sticks (1 cup) butter, softened
1 large egg
1½ teaspoons vanilla extract
1 teaspoon lemon extract
2 tablespoons fresh lemon juice
2½ teaspoons minced fresh lavender
1⅔ cups flour
1 teaspoon ground cinnamon
¼ teaspoon ground nutmeg
1 teaspoon baking soda
¼ teaspoon baking powder
¼ teaspoon salt
1½ cups quick-cooking oats
1 cup fresh blueberries

Preheat the oven to 350°F.

In an electric mixer with the appropriate mixing attachment, add the sugar, brown sugar, butter, egg, vanilla extract, lemon extract, lemon juice, and fresh lavender. Mix until combined.

In a separate bowl, combine the flour, cinnamon, nutmeg, baking soda, baking powder, and salt. Use a spoon to stir, then slowly add the dry ingredients to the mixer, along with the oats, and mix well. Add the blueberries and mix slowly to evenly distribute the berries without breaking them apart.

Line two cookie sheets with parchment paper. Shape appx 2 tablespoons of dough into a ball at a time, and arrange on the cookie sheets making sure to leave 1 inch apart. Place in the oven and bake for 10 to 12 minutes. Remove from the oven and let cool before serving.

FUN FACT Lavender is part of the mint family, and is known as a plant that calms people's nerves. In France, teachers used to keep crushed lavender in their classrooms to calm down nervous and disruptive students.

PEANUT BUTTER CUP POUND CAKE

(GLUTEN-FREE IF USING GLUTEN-FREE CAKE MIX)

This is the recipe I prepared for the segment of GE's *Our American Kitchen* that I was featured in. Like a lot of people, I love the combination of peanut butter and chocolate. So it's no surprise that peanut butter cups are one of my favorite candies. And sometimes having them with cake is even better! If you and the folks you know feel the same way, then keep the ingredients on hand for those times when the craving hits, or when you have unexpected guests and want to bake something special that's quick and sure to put a smile on everyone's face.

MAKES 1 CAKE

1 16-ounce box pound cake mix
1¼ cups mini peanut butter cups, divided
Vanilla ice cream (optional)

Preheat the oven to 350°F.

Spray a 9 x 5 x 3 inch loaf pan with cooking spray.

Prepare the pound cake according to the package instructions. Stir in 1 cup of the mini peanut butter cups. Pour the pound cake batter into the pan. Sprinkle the remaining 1/4 cup of the mini peanut butter cups evenly on top of the batter and bake in the oven until a toothpick inserted into the cake comes out clean, about 50 to 60 minutes. Remove the cake from the oven and let it cool. Remove it from the pan, slice, and serve with a scoop of vanilla ice cream, if desired.

PINEAPPLE EXPRESS CUPCAKES

This cupcake recipe was inspired by another Bailey family favorite, my grandma Karen's Pineapple Icebox Dessert. Along with the hunt for the $5 Egg, and the Easter baskets full of candies and prizes, Grandma Karen's dessert was something my mom, aunts, and uncles looked forward to every Easter. She chose that dessert because the flavors complemented the Easter ham so nicely, and it was easy to make for a lot of people. I decided to take the ingredients and flavors in the Pineapple Icebox Dessert and turn them into one of my favorite kinds of desserts—cupcakes. These pineapple, coconut, vanilla wafer cupcakes taste great and, needless to say, are a sentimental favorite of my family. For all of you tropical flavor lovers out there, I hope these cupcakes become one of your favorites as well.

MAKES ABOUT 20 CUPCAKES

1 16-ounce box vanilla cake mix (choose your favorite)
1 3½ ounce box vanilla pudding mix (choose your favorite)
1½ cups crushed pineapple, divided
1 cup unsweetened coconut flakes, divided
1 cup vanilla wafer crumbles
3–4 cups Buttercream Frosting (depending on how much frosting you prefer on your cupcakes) (recipe follows)

Preheat the oven to 350°F.

Line a cupcake pan with cupcake liners (or use nonstick spray). Follow the instructions on the vanilla cake mix box and the vanilla pudding mix box, to make the batter and the pudding. Add the pudding mixture to the batter and beat until well blended. Stir in 1 cup of the crushed pineapple and ½ cup of the coconut flakes. Fill each cupcake cup three-quarters of the way with the batter. Place in the oven and bake until a toothpick inserted into the cupcakes comes out clean, about 18 to 22 minutes. Remove from the oven and let cool. Frost the cupcakes with the Buttercream Frosting. Sprinkle the remaining ½ cup of coconut flakes and the vanilla wafer crumbles on the cupcakes, topping them with the remaining ½ cup of crushed pineapple.

BUTTERCREAM FROSTING

MAKES ABOUT 1-1/2 CUPS

½ cup butter, softened
2 teaspoons vanilla extract
4 cups powdered sugar
3–4 tablespoons milk

In a bowl, use a mixer to mix the butter and vanilla. Gradually mix in the powdered sugar. Add the milk 1 tablespoon at a time until the frosting reaches your desired consistency.

FUN FACT The word "pineapple" comes from the Spanish word "piña" meaning pine cone, which is what a pineapple kinda looks like. Pineapples are grown by cutting off the tops, drying out the tops for 2 days, and then planting them. It takes 2 years for one pineapple to grow from a single pineapple plant, and the planting and harvesting must all be done by hand. The famous Dole Plantation on Oahu, Hawaii is home to some of the world's best pineapple groves, and the Guinness World Records Largest Permanent Hedge Garden Maze since 2007.

SALTED BLUE WAVE SUGAR COOKIES

This may sound funny to you at first, but there's a lot of me in this recipe: I love salty and sweet mixed together; my favorite color is blue; I love swimming and going to the beach; and with a little help from a few friends, I baked and individually packaged over six hundred of these cookies for the guests at the Autism Speaks to Los Angeles Celebrity Chef Gala back in October 2015. At the event, I also delivered my first public speech as one of the celebrity guest speakers, and I was honored to be a celebrity chef assisting the popular and awesome executive chef Nick Shipp. Epic night! Epic Blue Wave Cookies.

MAKES ABOUT A BAKER'S DOZEN

2 sticks (1 cup) salted butter
1 cup granulated sugar
1 tablespoon brown sugar
1 egg
2 teaspoons vanilla extract
3 cups all-purpose flour
2 teaspoons baking powder
¼ teaspoon table salt
1 (1-ounce) bottle blue food coloring
1 tablespoons coarse-ground salt
2 tablespoons corn syrup or agave nectar syrup
Seashell Candies (or pre-bought seashell-shaped white chocolate candies) (recipe follows)

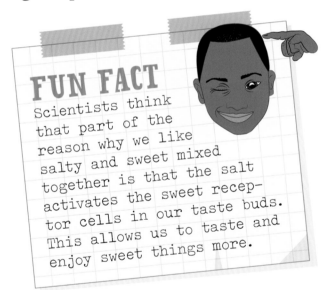

FUN FACT
Scientists think that part of the reason why we like salty and sweet mixed together is that the salt activates the sweet receptor cells in our taste buds. This allows us to taste and enjoy sweet things more.

Preheat the oven to 350°F.

Line a cookie sheet with parchment paper.

In a mixing bowl, combine the butter, sugar, brown sugar, egg, and vanilla. Mix until well blended. Next, add the flour, baking powder, and table salt, and mix until well blended. Add 5 to 7 drops of blue food coloring and mix until well blended. (Note: Add more or less food coloring depending on the color you're attempting to achieve.)

Roll the cookie dough into 2½-inch balls and arrange on the cookie sheet, allowing at least 2 inches of space between each ball. Flatten the tops slightly to make an even surface that will hold the coarse-ground salt. Sprinkle your desired amount of coarse-ground salt on top of each dough ball. Place in the oven and bake for 6 to 8 minutes. Remove from the oven and let cool.

Using a pastry brush, brush a bit of corn or agave nectar syrup on top of each cookie (to act as "glue"), then attach a seashell candy to each cookie.

SEASHELL CANDIES

MAKES APPROXIMATELY 12–15 CANDIES
12 ounces white chocolate candy melts

Fill a medium-sized saucepan one-third of the way to the top with water and place over medium heat.

Add the chocolate candy melts to a metal mixing bowl. Place the bowl over the saucepan (creating a double boiler) and let the heat from the hot water melt the chocolate, stirring occasionally. The chocolate should be warm, but not hot and runny. Remove from the heat and use a teaspoon to fill seashell-shaped candy molds, making sure not to overfill them.

COOL BREEZES & A SANTA ANA WIND

I think drinks are just as important as any other part of a meal. The right flavor and kind of drink can complement a meal and make it even more special, or enhance the theme of an event. A special drink can also be a treat all on its own. That's why in this chapter you will find different flavor mixes that include berries, citruses, melons, bananas, vegetables, florals, herbals, and spices; different temperatures—cold, room temperature, and hot; as well as different textures, including with and without pulp, light and thin, sparkly and fizzy, and thick, hearty smoothies.

FUN FACT Mixed drinks have been around for a long time. British sailors brought mixed drinks made with fruits from other lands back to Britain and the American colonies. Non-alcoholic mixed drinks became popular during the Victorian era because Queen Victoria did not approve of drinking alcohol, and it was considered especially inappropriate for women to do so. Having non-alcoholic drinks at events meant then, as it does today, that everyone could be included in the celebration and enjoy a drink that they didn't get to have every day.

BLUE MOON SMOOTHIE

(GLUTEN-FREE)

This is a great way to start off your morning, or to energize yourself at snack time. It's also perfect for people just starting out with non-dairy smoothies, and working their way up to the stronger-tasting power-smoothies that include sharp, tangy veggies and fruits. The fruity-nutty taste and texture of the blended blueberries, almonds, and coconut make this a great-tasting, nutrient-rich dairy-free drink. The color is pretty cool, too.

SERVES 4 TO 6

2½ cups dairy-free vanilla-flavored coconut yogurt
1 cup unsweetened vanilla-flavored almond milk
2 cups fresh blueberries
¼ cup raw or roasted unsalted almonds
2 cups ice

In a blender, add the yogurt, almond milk, blueberries, almonds, and ice. Blend on high until smooth, about 2 minutes, then serve.

Note: For a thicker smoothie, freeze the yogurt before blending.

FUN FACT Fruit smoothies showed-up on the scene during the 1940's, after inventor Frederick J. Osius and financial investor Fred Waring put the improved, modern electric blender on the market. It was called the "Miracle Mixer," but the name was later changed to the "Waring Blender." Fruit smoothies finally caught-on in the 1960's. During the 1990's, using frozen yogurt became popular to make smoothies thicker and creamier like milkshakes.

CHERRY CUCUMBER LIMEADE

(GLUTEN-FREE)

This was one of my first Cool Breezes drink recipes. The first time I served it, people were hooked and asked for more. Give the red fruit punch a rest and treat yourself to a glass of Cherry Cucumber Limeade instead. Cool, mellow, and not too sweet, this drink looks impressive and tastes delicious.

MAKES 4

2 (8-ounce) cans lemon-lime-flavored soda (choose your favorite)
1 cup maraschino cherry juice
20 fresh cherries, stemmed, pitted, and cut into quarters
10 cucumber slices, sliced again to resemble shreds
2 limes
8 ice cubes
4 cucumber slices, for garnish

In a medium size glass, combine 1 cup lime soda, 1/4 cup of the maraschino cherry juice, ¼ of the the cherries, and ¼ of the shredded cucumber. Squeeze the juice from ½ lime in the drink and add 2 ice cubes. Stir well to combine. Repeat with other 3 glasses. Garnish with a cucumber slice on the edge of each glass.

CINNA-PEACH TEA

(GLUTEN-FREE)

Eating and drinking fresh fruits in season is healthy for both our bodies and the planet, and it simply tastes better. When peach season rolls around, I like to celebrate with this cold, light peach drink that tastes a bit like a peach pie filling without the sugary calories. Enjoy this beverage all on its own as a delicious treat, or make a regular meal more fun by topping it off with this refreshing drink.

SERVES 6–8

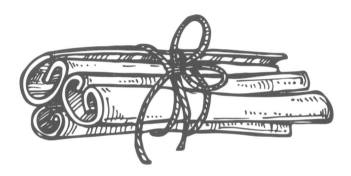

24 ounces peach nectar

10 cups water

3 large iced tea bags

¼ cup sugar

1 teaspoon ground cinnamon

4 ripe peaches, diced (if out of season, use diced canned peaches)

Pour the peach nectar into 1-ounce ice cube molds to make about 24 ice cubes. Place the molds in the freezer for 4 to 5 hours, or until frozen.

In a large pot, or teapot, bring 10 cups of water to a boil then remove from the heat. Pour the hot water into a heatproof pitcher. Add the tea bags; let steep for 6 to 10 minutes. Remove the tea bags and stir in the sugar and cinnamon. Add some ice and refrigerate for 3 to 4 hours.

To serve, pour ¼ cup of diced peaches in a glass, add 3 or 4 peach nectar ice cubes, and top off with the tea. Repeat the process with the remaining glasses.

HIGH-FIVIN' SUMMER DRINK

(GLUTEN-FREE)

What's great about this healthy summertime, or anytime, green drink is that it's the perfect disguise for broccoli, a vegetable that is full of nutrition but sometimes not that popular, especially not with kids. This drink is the only way my mom could get me to eat broccoli. In fact, if you're trying to get your kids to eat broccoli, maybe don't even tell them there's broccoli in this drink until they've finished. You can also pour the drink into fun glasses or mugs with cool straws and garnishes to make it even more appealing.

SERVES 4

1 cup fresh spinach
1 cup broccoli
1 small to medium-sized orange, peeled and chopped
½ banana, peeled and chopped
½ cup peeled and chopped fresh pineapple
2 cups apple juice
1 cup water

In a food processor, add the spinach, broccoli, orange, banana, pineapple, apple juice, and water. Blend on high until smooth.

FUN FACT

California produces most of the broccoli sold in the U.S. However, growing broccoli in the U.S. got its start on the East Coast, and was one of the many vegetables grown by President Thomas Jefferson in his vegetable garden at Monticello. Broccoli didn't catch-on in the U.S. until the 1920's, but it was popular in the Roman Empire thousands of years before that. In modern times, China produces more broccoli than any other country in the world.

MANDARIN VACATION

(GLUTEN-FREE)

I believe a lot of citrus drinks can be too strong or too sweet. I prefer a drink that has a nice citrus taste without the heavy flavors and sugars. This recipe lets you enjoy light citrus flavors complemented by bright, peppery basil. It's a refreshing drink for all occasions, but this one is especially good for cooling off during the summer.

SERVES 4

4 cups ice
6 mandarin oranges, peeled
1 cup fresh pineapple juice
¼ cup fresh papaya juice
¼ cup fresh mango juice
7–10 large basil leaves

In a blender, add the ice and blend to break down the chunks into bite-sized pieces, about 30 seconds. Add the oranges, the pineapple, papaya, and mango juices, and the basil leaves. Blend until the drink is a slushy consistency, about 1 minute. Do not overblend.

FUN FACT In Chinese, Japanese, English, Russian, and North American cultures, mandarin oranges are a symbol of abundance and good luck. In fact, mandarin oranges are traditionally given as gifts during Christmas and Chinese New Year.

MIDSUMMER NIGHT'S DREAM

(GLUTEN-FREE)

When I make this drink, a few thoughts come to mind. First, I like to combine aloe vera juice with fruit juices because aloe vera is a refreshing and healthy juice. Second, aloe vera juice has been around forever, but it's only now catching on with consumers as an everyday beverage option. Finally, I enjoy a drink with very little sugar. Many people are so used to the taste of super-sugary drinks that they don't realize just how much sugar is added to a lot of familiar fruit juices. Don't get me wrong, I like sugar as much as the next guy, but I try to watch how much I take in. Besides, too much sugar in a drink can get in the way of tasting the actual fruit. When you taste this drink, you'll notice immediately that it's not sugary and has a very pleasant, summertime flavor.

SERVES 4–6

20 strawberries, stems removed
1 cup cubed watermelon
1 cup cubed honeydew melon
3 cups aloe vera juice
1 cup water
2 tablespoon sugar
8 ice cubes

Cut five of the strawberries into quarters and set aside.

In a blender, add the remaining strawberries, watermelon, honeydew, aloe vera juice, water, and sugar. Blend on high until smooth. Pour into a pitcher and add the ice. Chill in the refrigerator for at least 1 hour before serving. Garnish with the cut strawberries.

PARADISE WATER

(GLUTEN-FREE)

This fruit-medley-flavored, no-sugar-added water is refreshing, healthy, and delicious. Light and filled with subtle flavors, this beverage complements many foods. The fruit adds a rainbow of color in a glass pitcher, a bowl, or especially a barrel dispenser that can serve as a decoration on the counter. The fresh ingredients I've listed are the fruits and vegetables I recommend, but feel free to experiment with your own combinations. This is also a good way to get both kids and adults to drink more water.

MAKES ABOUT 3 GALLONS

4 large apricots
2 large red apples
2 large navel oranges
1 lemon
1 medium cucumber
3 cups strawberries
3 gallons cold water

Cut the apricots in half and remove the pits. Using an apple corer, remove the cores of the apples. Cut each apple into eight slices. Leaving the peel of the oranges intact, remove the ends and slice each orange into six rings. Repeat the same procedure for the lemon, slicing it into four rings. Slice the cucumber into ¼-inch slices. Remove the stems from the strawberries and slice each berry in half. Add all of the fruit to a large barrel water dispenser. Add the water and fill the remaining space with ice. Let sit for 2 hours before serving.

PARFAIT YAY-YAY

The Parfait Yay-Yay is satisfying, super smooth, and slightly sweet without being too rich or heavy on your stomach. Banana, Greek yogurt, agave nectar, almond extract, strawberries, and granola all work together to nourish and energize you in a way that isn't bland or boring, making this smoothie perfect for a breakfast, snack, or dessert. In fact, you'll forget that it's actually good for you.

SERVES 3

2 cups chilled plain yogurt
2 cups chilled milk
2 small bananas
2 tablespoons agave syrup
1½ teaspoons non-alcoholic almond extract
1 teaspoon non-alcoholic vanilla extract
Strawberry Skewers, for garnish (recipe follows)

In a blender, add the yogurt, milk, bananas, agave syrup, almond extract, and vanilla extract. Blend until smooth. Garnish each serving with a Strawberry Skewer.

STRAWBERRY SKEWERS

MAKES 3 SKEWERS

½ cup peanut-butter-flavored granola
12 ounces white chocolate candy melts
1½ teaspoons ground cinnamon
9 medium-large sized strawberries

Line a cookie sheet with parchment paper.

In a shallow pan or bowl, add the granola.

Fill a medium-sized saucepan a third of the way to the top with water and place over medium heat.

Add the chocolate candy melts to a metal mixing bowl. Place the bowl over the saucepan (creating a double boiler) to allow the heat from the hot water to melt the chocolate, stirring occasionally. The chocolate should be warm, but not hot and runny. Stir in the cinnamon, and remove from the heat.

Dip the strawberries in the warm chocolate mixture to fully coat, then roll them in the granola. Place each strawberry on the parchment paper, and set in freezer for 10 to 15 minutes for the chocolate to harden. Remove from the freezer and insert three strawberries onto a cocktail skewer. Repeat with the other skewer.

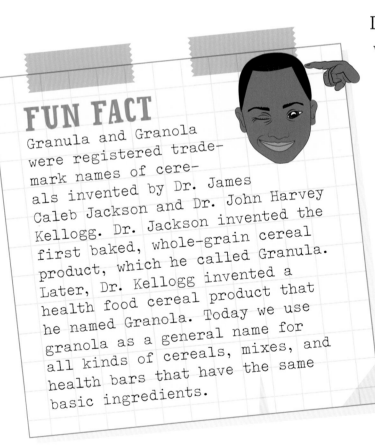

FUN FACT

Granula and Granola were registered trademark names of cereals invented by Dr. James Caleb Jackson and Dr. John Harvey Kellogg. Dr. Jackson invented the first baked, whole-grain cereal product, which he called Granula. Later, Dr. Kellogg invented a health food cereal product that he named Granola. Today we use granola as a general name for all kinds of cereals, mixes, and health bars that have the same basic ingredients.

PIZZERIA DRINK

(GLUTEN-FREE IF USING GLUTEN-FREE ENGLISH MUFFINS)

I enjoy all kinds of food, but pizza plus salad is still one of my favorite meals. This recipe is a hearty, family-friendly happy-hour show-stopper! Serve this savory vegetable drink, garnished with a pizza-on-a-skewer, in a mason jar for an impressive and fun party combo.

SERVES 3

2 medium-sized tomatoes
1 stalk celery, chopped
1 carrot, peeled and chopped
1 cup chopped romaine lettuce
¼ cup chopped green onions
½ red bell pepper, chopped
3 cups water
1 teaspoon salt
1 teaspoon Italian seasoning
Pizza Skewers, for garnish (recipe follows)

In a food processor, add the tomatoes, celery, carrot, lettuce, green onions, bell pepper, water, salt, and Italian seasoning. Blend on high for 2 to 3 minutes, or until smooth. Garnish with a pizza skewer.

PIZZA SKEWERS

MAKES 3 SKEWERS

3 English muffins
3 tablespoons olive oil
1 teaspoon garlic powder
11/2 cups shredded mozzarella
9 large pepperoni slices
9 fresh basil leaves

FUN FACT
Tomato juice is the official state beverage of Ohio. Twenty of the states have milk as their official beverage, and surprisingly only one state, Indiana, has water as its official beverage.

Preheat the oven to 350°F.

Slice the muffins in half and brush each one with olive oil. Sprinkle the garlic powder and mozzarella evenly on the muffins. Place the muffins on a cooking sheet and place in the oven. Bake for appx 8 minutes or until cheese has melted. Remove from oven and let cool slightly.

Using a 7-inch knotted skewer, spear one of the muffin halves, a pepperoni slice folded into quarters, and a basil leaf. Repeat and then rest the skewer on the rim of the glass, being careful that the food doesn't touch the drink. Repeat with the other skewers.

SANTA ANA WIND

(GLUTEN-FREE)

Those of us from Southern California and Baja California are familiar with the hot, dry winds that blow across the region at different times throughout the year. Known as Santa Ana winds, they're often the cause of spreading wildfires during the dangerous forest fire season. This is when hot is not my friend. But during the cooler times of the year, I enjoy hot drinks because they warm me up and remind me of holidays and seasonal activities and events. For me, this ginger milk recipe is all about comfort and good times. During the holidays, I like to add a dash of nutmeg for that extra seasonal flavor. I recommend the Sana Ana Wind as a great morning beverage for those who don't drink coffee, or a soothing evening drink before bedtime.

SERVES 2–4

4 cups milk
¼ teaspoon fresh vanilla seeds (slice open a fresh vanilla bean and use a knife to scrape out the seeds)
1 teaspoon minced fresh gingerroot
2 tablespoons honey
2 cinnamon sticks
¼ teaspoon ground nutmeg (optional)

In a medium-sized pot, heat the milk over low heat. Add the vanilla seeds, ginger, honey, and nutmeg, if desired.

Use a whisk to break up the vanilla seeds and mix the ingredients together. Add the cinnamon sticks and continue to let the milk mixture simmer on low for an additional 5 to 10 minutes, stirring occasionally. Remove from the heat and serve warm.

BONUS RECIPE
For Your Canine Companions

MIGHTY ALMIGHTY DOG TREATS

My dogs aren't just pets—they're a part of my family. I have a tan-and-white pit bull mix named Penelope, and a black-and-white pit bull mix named Tabitha. Like any other member of the family, they have their own personalities, and things they like and don't like. They love to be with us no matter what we're doing. They also love to eat. But like the rest of us, they can't eat whatever they want, whenever they want. Like many dogs (and people, of course), my dogs have food sensitivities, so I'm careful about what I feed them. Penelope and Tabitha require grain-free diets with lamb and lean beef proteins. I make sure their treats are healthy for them as well. One of their favorites is the Mighty Almighty Dog Treat recipe that I created for them. It's fresh, ground lamb mixed with black beans, peas, carrots, and cottage cheese, baked like a meat loaf. I cut it up into bite-sized pieces and give it to them a little at a time. They love this treat so much, they would probably eat the whole pan all at once if I let them. Staying active, hanging out with the rest of the family, and eating healthy delicious food helps them to live happy lives. If you have dogs in your family, I'm sure you want them to be happy, too. Also, make sure you're taking them to a good vet for regular checkups, and find out what foods are best for them before feeding them anything new.

1 pound lamb, uncooked
1/3 cup beef broth
1/3 cup cooked and mashed black beans
1/4 cup cooked and mashed peas
1/4 cup cooked and mashed carrots
1/2 cup cottage cheese

Preheat the oven to 375°F.

In a large mixing bowl, combine the lamb and beef broth. Add the black beans, peas, carrots, and cottage cheese. Mix well. Place the mixture in a casserole dish, spreading evenly. Bake for 45 minutes. Remove from the oven and let cool. Slice and serve as treats for your dog.

FUN FACT

The first dog biscuits were introduced in 1860; however, it's really only been in the last 60 years that the commercial dog food business exploded, which makes it something very new in human and canine history. Before that, dogs were fed table scraps, and / or whatever they could hunt or find on their own.

FUN FACTS REFERENCES

BREAKFAST: GET UP & GO

Breakfast in Asia. Mr. Breakfast Special Feature. Retrieved April 1, 2016.
http://www.mrbreakfast.com/w_asia.asp

History of Breakfast. (n.d.). In *Wikipedia*. Retrieved April 1, 2016.
https://en.wikipedia.org/wiki/History_of_breakfast

BANANA COCONUT CEREAL

The Golden Spurtle: World Porridge Day. Retrieved April 9, 2016.
http://www.goldenspurtle.com/

BARN YARD BREAKFAST MUFFINS

History of Muffin. Food History. Retrieved May 5, 2016.
http://www.world-foodhistory.com/2007/04/history-of-muffin.html

Muffins: A History. FoodReference.com. Retrieved. May 5, 2016.
http://www.foodreference.com/html/artmuffinhistory.html

PIGS IN A WAFFLE

Waffle History. The Nibble. Retrieved May 15, 2016.
http://www.thenibble.com/reviews/main/cereals/waffle-history.asp

Cornelius Swartwout. (n.d.) In Wikipedia. Retrieved May 15, 2016.
https://en.wikipedia.org/wiki/Cornelius_Swartwout

March 25th is International Waffle Day. Foodimentary / National Food Holidays. Retrieved May 15, 2016.
https://foodimentary.com/2014/03/25/march-25-is-international-waffle-day/

SLICE OF EGGCELLENCE (A.K.A. EGGCELLENCE BREAKFAST PIZZA)

Humanely Raised Eggs Cage Free vs Free Range: The Meaning of Free-Range, Cage-Free, and Other
Labels. verywell. verywell.com. Retrieved May 20, 2016.
https://www.verywell.com/what-is-a-cage-free-egg-2242153

Eggs – Free Range, Cage Free, Organic, What's The Difference? Dickison, Stephanie. Organic Lifestyle
Magazine. Retrieved May 20, 2016.
http://www.organiclifestylemagazine.com/issue/7-eggs-free-range-cage-free-organic-whats-the-difference

How Fresh Are Your Eggs? What's Cooking America? whatscookingamerica.net. Retrieved May 20, 2016.
http://whatscookingamerica.net/Q-A/EggsSell.htm

How Long Do Days Last? EATBYDATE. Eatbydate.com. Retrieved May 20, 2016.
http://www.Eatbydate.com/eggs-shelf-life-expiration-date/

SMOKED CHICKEN PANCAKES
Pancake Day. Castelow, Ellen. Historic UK: The History and Heritage Accommodation Guide. Retrieved April 10, 2016.
http://www.historic-uk.com/CultureUK/Pancake-Day/

Shrove Tuesday. (n.d.). In Wikipedia. Retrieved April 10, 2016.
https://en.wikipedia.org/wiki/Shrove_Tuesday

STUFFED HASH POTATO
George Washington Carver. (n.d.) In Wikipedia. Retrieved May 20, 2016.
https://en.wikipedia.org/wiki/George_Washington_Carver#Sweet_potato_products

Carver Sweet Potato Products. Tuskegee University. Tuskegee.edu. Retrieved May, 20, 2016.
http://www.tuskegee.edu/about_us/legacy_of_fame/george_w_carver/carver_sweet_potato_products.aspx

SUNSHINE MUFFINS
Cranberry Trivia. The Old Farmer's Almanac. almanac.com. Retrieved May 18, 2016.
http://www.almanac.com/content/cranberry-trivia

Cranberries: Cranberry Trivia. Food Reference. foodreference.com. Retrieved May 18, 2016.
http://www.foodreference.com/html/fcranberries.html

SWEET FRENCH BREAKFAST
Frenchless Toast. FoodReference.com. Retrieved on April 10, 2016.
http://www.foodreference.com/html/a-french-toast-history.html

The History of French Toast. The Spydersden. Retrieved April 10, 2016.
https://spydersden.wordpress.com/2013/01/24/the-history-of-french-toast/

LUNCH: FEED THE BEAST
How Long is Your Lunch Break? Le Billon, Karen. karenlebillon.com. Retrieved April 8, 2016.
https://karenlebillon.com/2011/10/16/how-long-is-your-lunch-break-in-france-its-two-hours/

Lunch. (n.d.) In Wikipedia. Retrieved April 8, 2016.
https://en.wikipedia.org/wiki/Lunch

CAVEMAN KABOBS
Did You Know: Food History – On Shish Kebabs. CliffordAWright.com. Retrieved on April 10, 2016.
www.cliffordawright.com/caw/food/entries/display.php/id/82

Kebab. (n.d.). In Wikipedia. Retrieved April 10, 2016.
https://en.wikipedia.org/wiki/Kabob

FISH SUB
The Origin of Hoagies, Grinders, Subs, Heroes, and Spuckies. Bon Appetit. Retrieved June 21, 2016
http://www.bonappetit.com/test-kitchen/ingredients/article/the-origin-of-hoagies-grinders-subs-heroes-and-spuckies

Muffuletta Sandwich Recipe - History of Muffuletta Sandwich. What's Cooking America? Retrieved June 21, 2016.
whatscookingamerica.net/History/Sandwiches/Muffuletta.htm

Submarine Sandwich. (n.d.) In Wikipedia. Retrieved June 21, 2016.
https://en.wikipedia.org/wiki/Submarine_sandwiches

GRILLED CHICKEN PANINI
Thomas Edison Invented This Early Panini Press. Spector, Dina / Business Insider. SFGate. Retrieved April 19, 2016.
http://www.sfgate.com/technology/businessinsider/article/Thomas-Edison-Invented-This-Early-Panini-Press-4660383.php

HEARTY CHICKEN & LEMON VERBENA SOUP
Lemon Verbena. the epicentre. epicentre.com. Retrieved May 18, 2016.

Live Naturally With Herbs. East, Katherine. Natural News. naturalnews.com. Retrieved May 18, 2016.
http://www.naturalnews.com/026543_tea_oil_herb.html

KICK BACK PEPPER JACK
The Stories of Monterey Jack. Real California Milk. Retrieved April 11, 2016.
http://www.realcaliforniamilk.com/recipes/#recipes-browser/overlay/406

Pepper Jack. Cheese.com. Retrieved April 11, 2016.
http://www.cheese.com/pepper-jack/

MUSHROOM GRAVY SLIDERS
Mind-Boggling Facts About Mushrooms. United States Department of Agriculture Services. Ars.usda.gov. Retrieved April 29, 2016.
http://www.ars.usda.gov/is/kids/farm/story4/mushroomfacts.htm

The Mushroom Story: History and Background. freshmushrooms: nature's hidden treasures. mushroom-info.com. Retrieved April 29, 2016.
http://www.mushroominfo.com/history-and-background/

ORANGE WEDGE SALAD
Fact of the Day – Oranges. Top Food Facts. Retrieved April 9, 2016.
http://topfoodfacts.com/fact-of-the-day-oranges/
Fun Facts About Oranges. Oranges.com. Retrieved April 9, 2016.
http://oranges.com/fun-facts-about-oranges

SALMON SALAD SANDWICH
Wild Salmon vs Farm Salmon. Prevention Health Food Face-Off. Prevention.com. Retrieved April 29, 2016.
http://www.prevention.com/content/which-healthier-wild-salmon-vs-farmed-salmon

Smoked Salmon Candy. Shaw, Hank. Honest Food. honest-food.net. Retrieved April 29, 2016.
http://honest-food.net/2013/07/15/salmon-candy-recipe/

VEGAN BLACK BEAN CHILI & SPICY CHEESY CORN BREAD
National Chili Day. nationalchiliday.com. Retrieved April 29, 20
About ICS. International Chili Society. chilicookoff.com. Retrieved April 29, 2016.
http://www.chilicookoff.com/History/History_of_ICS.asp

Traditional Southern New Year's Day Dinner. Rattray, Diana. About Food. Aboutfood.com. Retrieved April 10, 2016.
http://southernfood.about.com/od/holidayandpartyrecipes/a/newyearsdinner.htm

Southern Perspective: New Year's Day Menu is Key. Davis, Linda A.B. Pensacola Journal / USA Today Network. Retrieved April 10, 2016.
http://www.pnj.com/story/life/2014/12/27/linda-davis-column/20953837/

SNACKS: PICK-ME-UPS
History of High Tea – History Afternoon Tea. whatscookingamerica.net. Retrieved April 8, 2016
http://whatscookingamerica.net/History/HighTeaHistory.htm

High Tea, Afternoon Tea, Elevenses: English Tea Times for Dummies. Whitehead, Nadia. NPR. The Salt: What's on Your Plate. Retrieved April 8, 2016.
http://www.npr.org/sections/thesalt/2015/06/30/418660351/high-tea-afternoon-tea-elevenses-english-tea-times-for-dummies

APRICOT AMAZEBALLS
Food Symbolism – Chinese Customs During Chinese New Year
www.nationsonline.org/oneworld/Chinese_Customs/food_symbolism.htm

Apricot. (n.d.). In Wikipedia. Retrieved April 10, 2016.
https://en.wikipedia.org/wiki/Apricot

HEIRLOOM TOMATO BASIL SALAD WITH PARMESAN CRISPS
Food Facts: Tomato Facts for Kids. Science Kids: Fun Facts and Science for Kids. Retrieved April 9, 2016.
http://www.sciencekids.co.nz/sciencefacts/food/tomatoes.html

Vine Ripe Pink Tomato: Arkansas State Fruit & Vegetable. State Symbols USA. Retrieved April, 9 2016.
http://www.statesymbolsusa.org/symbol-official-item/arkansas/state-food-agriculture-symbol/south-arkansas-vine-ripe-pink-tomato

HUMMUS OF OLYMPUS
Who Invented Hummus? Horan, Mike & Chrissy. STRAIGHT DOPE. straightdope.com. Retrieved May 12, 2016.
http://www.straightdope.com/columns/read/1898/who-invented-hummus

Hummus! The Movie. hummustheovie.com. Retrieved May 12, 2016.
http://www.hummusthemovie.com/

Largest Serving of Hummus in the World. Guinness World Records. guinnessworldrecords.com. Retrieved May 12, 2016.
http://www.guinnessworldrecords.com/world-records/largest-serving-of-hummus/
http://www.hummusthemovie.com/

NACHO MI TACO
Rebecca Webb Carranza, 98; Pioneered Creation, Manufacture of Tortilla Chip: Nelson, Valerie. Los Angeles Times. Retrieved April 8, 2016.
http://articles.latimes.com/2006/feb/07/local/me-carranza7

Tortilla Chip. (n.d.). In Wikipedia. Retrieved April 8, 2016.
https://en.wikipedia.org/wiki/Tortilla

PEACHY KEEN
Donut Peach. Harvest to Table. Retrieved April 10, 2016.
http://www.harvesttotable.com/2008/05/doughnut_peach/

Saturn Peach. (n.d.) In Wikipedia. Retrieved April 10, 2016.
https://en.wikipedia.org/wiki/Saturn_peach

PEANUT BUTTER, NUTELLA®, & APPLE (PBNA) PANINI
World Nutella Day: 10 Things You Didn't Know About the Chocolate Spread. The Telegraph. Retrieved April 10, 2016.
http://www.telegraph.co.uk/food-and-drink/features/world-nutella-day-10-things-you-didnt-know-about-the-choc-spread/

Nutella. (n.d.) In Wikipedia. Retrieved April 10, 2016.
https://en.wikipedia.org/wiki/Nutella

SPICY DOUBLE-DIPPED ONION STRAWS
Why Do Onions Make You Cry? Helmenstine, Anne Marie, PHD. about education. About.com. Retrieved April 8, 2016.
http://chemistry.about.com/od/chemistryfaqs/f/onionscry.htm

Why Do Onions Make Us Cry? The Human Touch of Chemistry. Retrieved April 8, 2016.
http://www.humantouchofchemistry.com/why-do-onions-make-us-cry.htm

DINNER: LET'S FEAST
Difference Between Dinner & Supper. DifferenceBetween.net. Retrieved April 8, 2016.
http://www.differencebetween.net/language/difference-between-supper-and-dinner/

Dining Customs of Different Cultures. familyeducation.com. Retrieved April 8, 2016.
http://life.familyeducation.com/cross-cultural-relations/behavior/48976.html

Dinner is at What Time? The Argentine Eating Schedule. Parrilla Tour Buenos Aires. Retrieved April 8, 2016. https://parrillatour.com/dinner-is-at-what-time-the-argentine-eating-schedule/

BAKED TILAPIA & VEGGIE POTATO ALMIGHTY
Tilapia. (n.d.) In Wikipedia. Retrieved May 15, 2016.
https://en.wikipedia.org/wiki/Tilapia

Tilapia as a Sacred Symbol. samlib.ru. Retrieved May 15, 2016.
http://samlib.ru/a/amelxkin_a_a/symbol.shtml

Hathor. (n.d.) In Wikipedia. Retrieved May 15, 2016.
https://en.wikipedia.org/wiki/Hathor

Space Spuds to the Rescue. NASA. nasa.gov. Retrieved May 15, 2016.
http://www.nasa.gov/vision/earth/everydaylife/spacespuds.html

Growing Plants and Vegetables in a Space Garden. NASA. nasa.gov. Retrieved May 15, 2016.

CHICKEN AND VEGGIE VERDE ENCHILADAS
Enchiladas Fun Facts. Myrick, Richard. Mobile Cuisine. Retrieved April 19, 2016.
http://mobile-cuisine.com/did-you-know/enchilada-fun-facts/

Short History of Enchiladas. Hacked by ReFLex. bighistory.net. Retrieved April 19, 2016.
http://www.bighistory.net/short-history-of-enchilada/

FISH-AND-CHIPS

25 Mouthwatering Facts About Fish & Chips. Malone, Ailbhe. BuzzFeed. Retrieved April 19, 2016.
https://www.buzzfeed.com/ailbhemalone/absolutely-mouthwatering-facts-about-fish-and-chips?utm_term=.wjmzAKepG4#.uu3eqW1X54

The National Fish & Chip Awards. Fishandchipawards.com. Retrieved April 19, 2016.
http://www.fishandchipawards.com/

GRILLED PORTOBELLO RICE BOWL

The History of Teriyaki Sauce. Katemopoulos, Maureen. eHow Food & Drink. ehow.com. Retrieved May 18, 2016.
http://www.ehow.com/about_5251710_history-teriyaki-sauce.html

Teriyaki. (n.d.) In Wikipedia. Retrieved May 18, 2016.
https://en.wikipedia.org/wiki/Teriyaki

MEXI-BURGERS

Facts on Cumin. The Great American Spice Company. Retrieved April 9, 2016.
http://blog.americanspice.com/index.php/fun-facts-on-cumin/

Cumin. FoodReference.com. Retrieved April 9, 2016
http://www.foodreference.com/html/fcumin.html

PAPA BURGER

25 Amazing Facts About Burgers. MSN. Retrieved June 21, 2016.
w.msn.com/.../foodnews/25-amazing-facts-about-burgers/ss-BBjBWiQ

Americans Eat How Many Burgers A Year? Huffington Post. Retrieved June 21, 2016.
www.huffingtonpost.com/2013/07/28/burger-facts-trivia_n_3654636.html

Hamburger. (n.d.) In Wikipedia. Retrieved June 21, 2016.
https://en.wikipedia.org/wiki/Beefburger

SLOPPY CHASE WITH LAMB

Sloppy Joe. (n.d.) In Wikipedia. Retrieved May 11, 2016.
https://en.wikipedia.org/wiki/Sloppy_joe

Rou Ji Amo. (n.d.) In Wikipedia. Retrieved. May 11, 2016.
https://en.wikipedia.org/wiki/Roujiamo

STRONG & SPICY BURGER

Sriracha Hot Sauce Purveyor Turns Up the Heat. Shyong, Frank. Los Angeles Times. Retrieved April 8, 2016.
articles.latimes.com/2013/apr/12/business/la-fi-himi-tran-20130414

Making the Most of Sriracha Sauce. Moncel, Bethany. about food. Retrieved April 8, 2016.
http://foodreference.about.com/od/Ethnic_Ingredients/a/Sriracha-Sauce.htm

TIKKA MASALA PIZZA

A Brief History of Chicken Masala. Food Detective's Diary. Retrieved April 19, 2016.
http://fooddetectivesdiary.blogspot.com/2011/02/brief-history-of-chicken-tikka-masala.html

The History of Your Favourite Curry - Chicken Tikka Masala. EastZEast: The Home of Punjabi Cooking. Retrieved April 19, 2016.

VEGGIE-GHETTI

Symbolic Foods of Chinese New Year. Butler, Stephanie. Hungry History. History.com. Retrieved April 11, 2016.
http://www.history.com/news/hungry-history/symbolic-foods-of-chinese-new-year

Top Symbolic Chinese Foods: From Fish to Fowl. about food. About.com. Retrieved April 11, 2016.
http://chinesefood.about.com/od/foodfestivals/tp/foodsymbolism.htm

The History of Noodles: How a Simple Food Became a Worldwide Symbol. McDonnell, Justin. The Atlantic. Retrieved April 11, 2016.
http://www.theatlantic.com/china/archive/2013/08/the-history-of-noodles-how-a-simple-food-be-came-a-worldwide-staple/278637/

The History of Noodles: How a Simple Food Became a Worldwide StapleThe History of Noodles: How a Simple Food Became a Worldwide Staple

DESSERT: LIFE IS SWEET

History of Desserts. Delp, Valerie. Love to Know. Retrieved April 8, 2016.
http://gourmet.lovetoknow.com/History_of_Desserts

Dessert. (n.d.) In Wikipedia. Retrieved April 8, 2016.
https://en.wikipedia.org/wiki/Dessert#Usage

BANANA SPLIT MINI MOIST CAKES

The Story Behind the Banana Split. Lifestyle. AOL.com. Retrieved April 11, 2016.
http://www.aol.com/food/story-behind-banana-split/

Who Invented the Banana Split? Attoun, Marti. American Profile. Retrieved April 11, 2016.

BROWNIE S'MORES SANDWICHES

Mallomars: The Cookie Everyone Likes to Hoard. The Salt: What's On Your Plate. NPR. Retrieved April 9, 2016
http://www.npr.org/sections/thesalt/2013/11/17/244158182/mallomars-the-cookie-everyone-likes-to-hoard

About MoonPie. MoonPie.com. Retrieved April 9, 2016.
http://moonpie.com/about

S'more. (n.d.). In Wikipedia. Retrieved April 9, 2016.
https://en.wikipedia.org/wiki/S'more

COCA-COLA® CAKE

World Chocolate Day: 10 Weird Chocolate Facts. Alexander, Saffron. The Telegraph. Retrieved April 10, 2016.
http://www.telegraph.co.uk/foodanddrink/foodanddrinknews/11722935/World-Chocolate-Day-10-weird-chocolate-facts.html

Did You Know That The Chocolate River in Willy Wonka and The Chocolate Factory Was Made From Real Chocolate? Facts WT: The Best Knowledge Source. Retrieved April 10, 2016.
http://www.factswt.com/did-you-know-that-the-chocolate-river-in-willy-wonka-and-the-chocolate-fac-tory-was-made-from/

FESTIVE PRETZEL SALAD

16 Fascinating Facts About Jell-O. Epstein, Leonora. BuzzFeed. Retrieved April 10, 2016.
www.buzzfeed.com/leonoraepstein/16-fascinating-facts-about-jell-o

Jell-O. (n.d.). In Wikipedia. Retrieved April 10, 2016.
https://en.wikipedia.org/wiki/Jell-O

GRANDMA KAREN'S GINGERBREAD
25 Amazing Facts About Ginger You Never Knew. Amazing and Weird Facts. Retrieved April 10, 2016.
www.amazingandweird.com/facts/25-interesting-facts-ginger-never-knew
History of Ginger. In Depth Info On Ginger. Retrieved April 10, 2016.
www.indepthinfo.com/ginger/history.shtml

LEMONADER
Guinness World Record: Heaviest Lemon. Guinness World Records. Retrieved April 9, 2016.
http://www.guinnessworldrecords.com/world-records/heaviest-lemon/

NOT YOUR AVERAGE OATMEAL COOKIE
10 Interesting Lavender Facts. The Village Shops on Venetian Bay. Retrieved April 10, 2016.
http://www.venetianvillage.com/10-interesting-lavender-facts/

Interesting Facts About Lavender. Just Fun Facts. Retrieved April 10, 2016.
http://justfunfacts.com/interesting-facts-about-lavender/

PINEAPPLE EXPRESS CUPCAKES
Pineapple Facts for Kids. Food Facts. Science Kids. Retrieved May 15, 2016.
http://www.sciencekids.co.nz/sciencefacts/food/pineapples.html

Fun Pineapple Facts. King of Fruit. Retrieved May 15, 2016.
http://www.kingoffruit.com.au/fun-pineapple-facts.html

James Dole. (n.d.) In Wikipedia. Retrieved May 15, 2016.

SALTED BLUE WAVE SUGAR COOKIE
Scientists Find Why Sweet And Salty Pair So Sweetly. delish.com. Retrieved April 10, 2016.
http://www.delish.com/food/news/a38571/the-science-behind-sweet-and-salty-pairings/

Sweet and Salty. The Frontal Cortex. Retrieved April 9, 2016.
http://scienceblogs.com/cortex/2009/07/01/sweet-and-salty-1/

DRINKS: COOL BREEZES & A SANTA ANA WIND
The Surprising History of Punch. Hungry History. History.com. Retrieved April 8, 2016.
http://www.history.com/news/hungry-history/the-surprising-history-of-punch

BLUE MOON SMOOTHIE
The Blender – History of the Kitchen Blender. Inventors. theinventors.org. Retrieved May 15, 2016.
http://theinventors.org/library/inventors/blblender.htm

Fred Waring. (n.d.) In Wikipedia. Retrieved May 15, 2010.
https://en.wikipedia.org/wiki/Fred_Waring

Smoothie History. Smoothie Recipe TV. smoothierecipetv.com. Retrieved May 15, 2016.
http://smoothierecipe.tv/smoothie-history/

CINNA-PEACH TEA
Fun Peach Facts. Cooper Farms. Cooperpeaches.com. Retrieved April 30, 2016.
https://cooperpeaches.com/peach-fun-facts/

Fruit: A History of Peaches. Hobby Farms. hobbyfarms.com. Retrieved April 30. 2016.
http://www.hobbyfarms.com/fruit-a-history-of-peaches/

Which State Grows the Most Peaches? Reference. Retrieved April 30, 2016.
https://www.reference.com/food/state-grows-peaches-529898cdae43a181#

Top 10 Producers of Peach in the World. Which Country? whichcountry.com. Retrieved April 30, 2016.
http://www.whichcountry.co/top-10-largest-producers-of-peach-in-the-world/

HIGH-FIVIN' SUMMER DRINK
10 Facts You May Not Know About Broccoli. Lewis, Leslie. Mindbodygreen. Retrieved April 20, 2016.
http://www.mindbodygreen.com/0-6039/10-Fun-Facts-You-May-Not-Know-About-Broccoli.html

Jefferson: The Scientist and Gardner. The Jefferson Monticello. monticello.org. Retrieved. April, 20, 2016.
https://www.monticello.org/site/house-and-gardens/jefferson-scientist-and-gardener

Broccoli. (n.d.) In Wikipedia. Retrieved April 20, 2016.
https://en.wikipedia.org/wiki/Broccoli

MANDARIN VACATION
Mandarin Oranges Symbol of Good Fortune. The Inspiration Shots. Retrieved April 19, 2016.
https://theinspirationshots.com/2016/02/18/mandarin-oranges-symbol-of-good-fortune/

Tangerines and Oranges: Chinese New Year Symbols. Cultural China. Retrieved April 19, 2016.
http://traditions.cultural-china.com/en/214T11982T14619.html

Mandarin Orange. (n.d.) In Wikipedia. Retrieved April 19, 2016.
https://en.wikipedia.org/wiki/Mandarin_orange#Cultural_significance

PARFAIT YAY-YAY
Granola Fun Facts. Mobile Cuisine. Retrieved April 29, 2016.
http://mobile-cuisine.com/did-you-know/granola-fun-facts/

Granola Origins and History. FoodReference.com. Retrieved April 29, 2016.
http://www.foodreference.com/html/artgranola.html

A History of Granola. Granola Delights. From Wikipedia. Retrieved April 29, 2016.
http://www.granoladelights.com/recipe/history_granola_wikipedia.htm

PIZZERIA DRINK
Tomato Juice: Ohio State Beverage. State Symbols USA. Retrieved April 19, 2016.
http://www.statesymbolsusa.org/symbol-official-item/ohio/state-food-agriculture-symbol/tomato-juice

List of U.S. State Beverages. (n.d.) In Wikipedia. Retrieved April 19, 2016
https://en.wikipedia.org/wiki/List_of_U.S._state_beverages

MIGHTY ALMIGHTY DOG TREATS
The History of the Pet Food Industry. Wolf, Alyssa. Pet Shops. about home. About.com. Retrieved June 12, 2016.
http://petshops.about.com/od/petfood/p/History-of-Pet-Food.htm

INDEX

Note: *Italicized* page numbers indicate "fun facts"; **bolded** numbers indicate photos.
Recipes followed by (GF) are gluten-free.

NOTES